D1123254

Discover Your
IQ
POTENTIAL

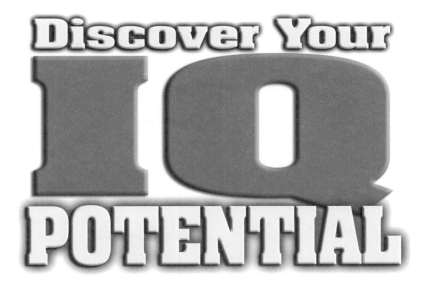

Ken Russell & Philip Carter

BARNES & NOBLE BOOKS

NEW YORK

This edition published by Barnes & Noble, Inc.
by arrangement with
Arcturus Publishing Limited
1–7 Shand Street
London SE1 2ES

2003 Barnes & Noble Books

M 10 9 8 7 6 5 4 3 2 1

All rights reserved. No part of this publication may be reproduced, stored in a retrieval system, or transmitted, in any form or by any means electronic, mechanical, photocopying, recording or otherwise, without written permission in accordance with the provisions of the Copyright Act 1956 (as amended). Any person or persons who do any unauthorized act in relation to this publication may be liable to criminal prosecution and civil claims for damages.

Copyright © Arcturus Publishing Limited

ISBN 0-7607-3434-8

Text design by Gary Everest
Cover design by Commuiniqué
Printed and bound in China

Welcome to **Discover Your IQ Potential**, a book packed with every sort of puzzle – word, number, and visual – designed to enhance your aptitude and stimulate your mind.

The book is divided into 20 sections, each containing 25 puzzles. No specialist knowledge is required to work them out. They can all be solved using standard mathematical or alphabetical calculations. Neither do the questions increase in difficulty as the book progresses. Hard and easy questions are randomly interspersed. So if you can't get one, don't despair! Just move on to the next question.

All the answers are listed at the back of the book, but we suggest that you don't look at them until you absolutely have to!

We have also provided some tables at the beginning of the book, which you may find a useful aid when tackling the puzzles.

Discover Your IQ Potential is a stimulating, challenging, but above all, fun way of sharpening your wits and training your mind to think logically.

We hope you enjoy it!

Numerical values		
A	1	26
B	2	25
C	3	24
D	4	23
E	5	22
F	6	21
G	7	20
H	8	19
I	9	18
J	10	17
K	11	16
L	12	15
M	13	14
N	14	13
O	15	12
P	16	11
Q	17	10
R	18	9
S	19	8
T	20	7
U	21	6
V	22	5
W	23	4
X	24	3
Y	25	2
Z	26	1

Multiplication Table

×	1	2	3	4	5	6	7	8	9	10	11	12
1	1	2	3	4	5	6	7	8	9	10	11	12
2	2	4	6	8	10	12	14	16	18	20	22	24
3	3	6	9	12	15	18	21	24	27	30	33	36
4	4	8	12	16	20	24	28	32	36	40	44	48
5	5	10	15	20	25	30	35	40	45	50	55	60
6	6	12	18	24	30	36	42	48	54	60	66	72
7	7	14	21	28	35	42	49	56	63	70	77	84
8	8	16	24	32	40	48	56	64	72	80	88	96
9	9	18	27	36	45	54	63	72	81	90	99	108
10	10	20	30	40	50	60	70	80	90	100	110	120
11	11	22	33	44	55	66	77	88	99	110	121	132
12	12	24	36	48	60	72	84	96	108	120	132	144

	Square Numbers	Cube Numbers
1	1	1
2	4	8
3	9	27
4	16	64
5	25	125
6	36	216
7	49	343
8	64	512
9	81	729
10	100	1000
11	121	1331
12	144	1728
13	169	2197
14	196	2744
15	225	3375
16	256	4096
17	289	4913
18	324	5832
19	361	6859
20	400	8000

Prime Numbers
2
3
5
7
11
13
17
19
23
29

PUZZLE 1

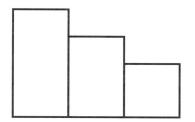 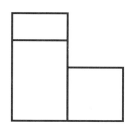 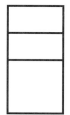 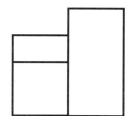

What comes next?

A   B   C

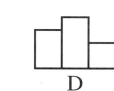

D   E

PUZZLE 2

How many minutes before 12 noon is it if 72 minutes ago it was twice as many minutes past 9 am?

PUZZLE 3

What number should replace the question mark?

4	5	1
2	?	5
4	2	4

S
E
C
T
I
O
N
1

PUZZLE 4

Frank has half as many again as Sally who has half again as many again as Mary. Altogether they have 209.

How many has each?

PUZZLE 5

What comes next in this sequence?

346

289

134

628

?

PUZZLE 6

 is to: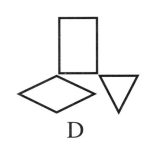

as:  is to:

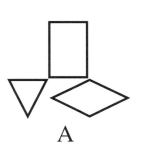
A

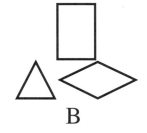
B

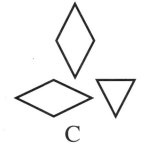
C

D

PUZZLE 7

What should replace the question mark?

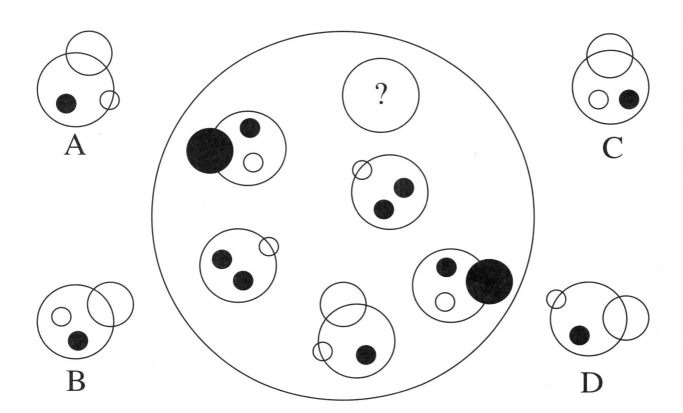

A

B

C

D

PUZZLE 8

**SUNDAY
MONDAY
TUESDAY
WEDNESDAY
THURSDAY
FRIDAY
SATURDAY**

What day comes two days after the day immediately before the day three days after the day immediately before the day which comes two days after Sunday?

PUZZLE 9

What number should replace the question mark?

7	8	9
4	6	8
1	?	7

PUZZLE 10

  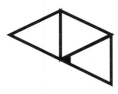

What comes next?

A

B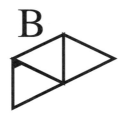

C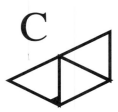

D

E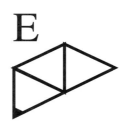

PUZZLE 11

What number should replace the ?

17			44
13	14	20	19

62			23

9	12	?	9
11			32

40			13

PUZZLE 12

What number should replace the ?

7	6	5	23
9	2	8	7
6	14	2	22
4	8	7	?

Each line and symbol which appears in the four outer circles, below, is transferred to the centre circle according to these rules: If a line or symbol occurs in the outer circles: once: it is transferred twice: it is possibly transferred   3 times: it is transferred   4 times: it is not transferred. Which of the circles A, B, C, D or E, should appear at the centre of the diagram, below?

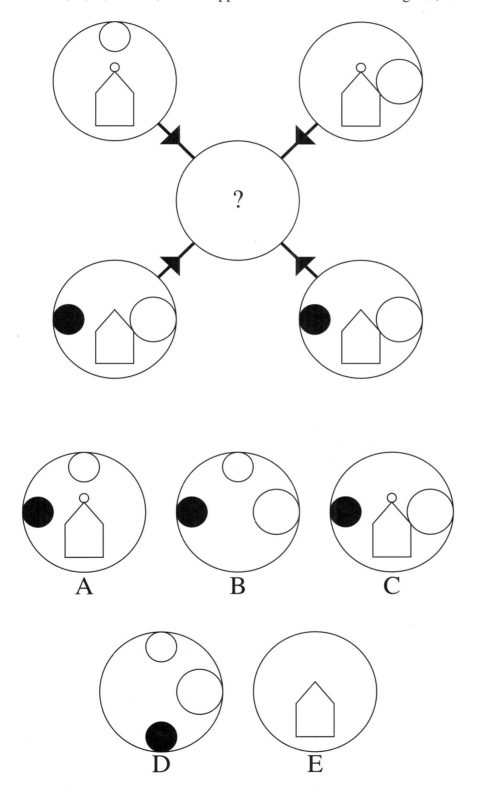

PUZZLE
14

| 1 | 7 | 9 | 8 | 2 | 0 | 6 |

is to:

| 9 | 6 | 0 | 2 | 1 | 7 | 8 |

as:

| 9 | 8 | 2 | 6 | 0 | 1 | 7 |

is to:

| 1 | 8 | 7 | 0 | 9 | 6 | 2 | | 0 | 2 | 1 | 8 | 7 | 9 | 6 |

| 7 | 2 | 1 | 6 | 0 | 9 | 8 | | 6 | 8 | 7 | 1 | 9 | 2 | 0 |

PUZZLE
15

Which wave A, B, C or D replaces the ?

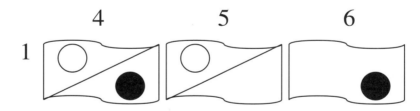

Which circle A, B, C, or D should replace the ?

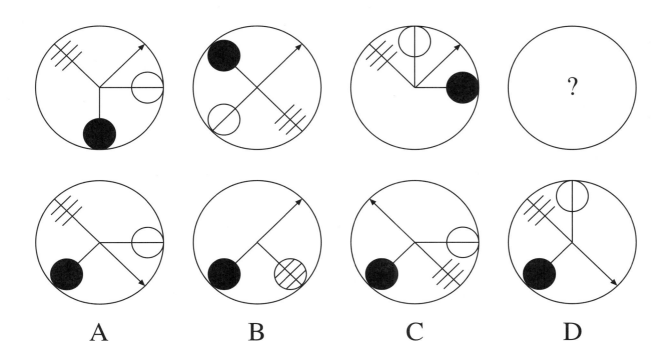

A   B   C   D

Which word is the same or closest in meaning to TORPID?

(a) TORPEDO LIKE
(b) MAGIC
(c) SLUGGISH
(d) ANCIENT
(e) KIND

A man drives to town 30 miles away at a speed of 45 mph and arrives in 40 mins. On his return he takes 60 mins. What is his average speed for the total trip?

SECTION 1

PUZZLE 19

Which circle is nearest in content to A?

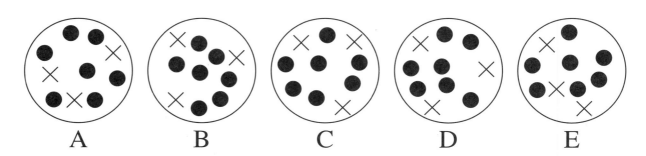

A   B   C   D   E

PUZZLE 20

What number should replace the ?

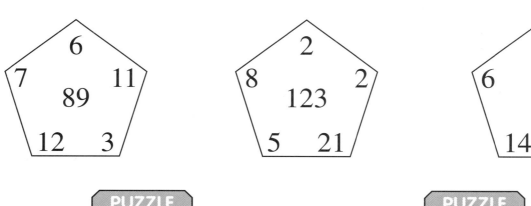

6
7   11
89
12   3

2
8   2
123
5   21

7
6   2
?
14   4

PUZZLE 21

Which one is the odd one out?

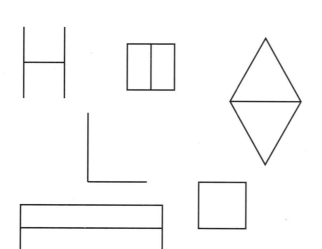

PUZZLE 22

Simplify

16 - 20 x 2 + 40 ÷ 8 + 19 = x

PUZZLE 23

Which word is the same or closest in meaning to TENUITY

(a) SOUNDLESS
(b) ACIDITY
(c) LICENCE
(d) BOLDNESS
(e) SLENDERNESS

Each of the nine squares in the grid marked A1 to C3, should incorporate all the lines and symbols which are shown in the squares of the same letter and number above and to the left. For example, B2 should incorporate all the lines and symbols that are in 2 and B. One of the squares is incorrect. Which one is it?

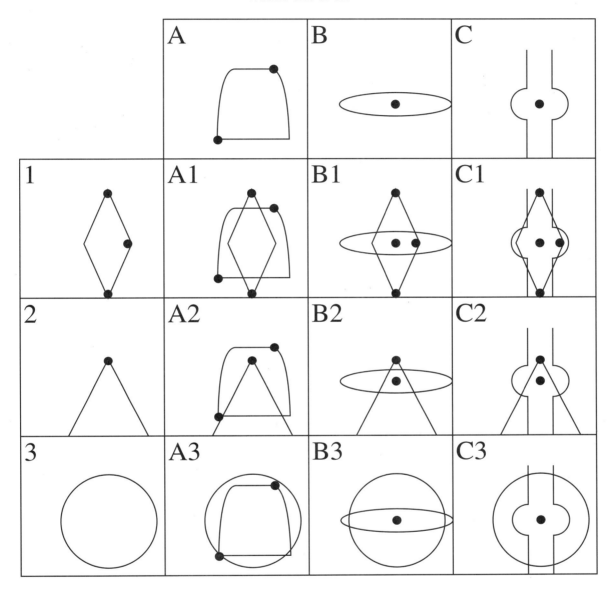

PUZZLE
25

What does PETTIFOGGING mean?

(a) LOSING DIRECTION

(b) AGGRESSIVENESS

(c) QUIBBLING

(d) GETTING LOST

Which is the missing segment?

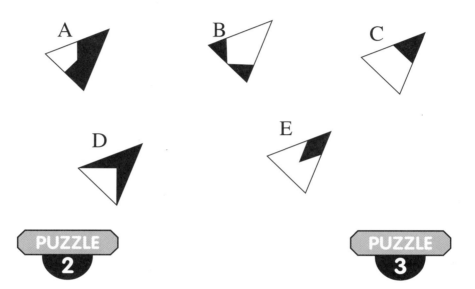

A

B

C

D

E

PUZZLE 2

Fill the grid with the letters ABCDE so that the same letter does not appear in the same horizontal, vertical or diagonal line.

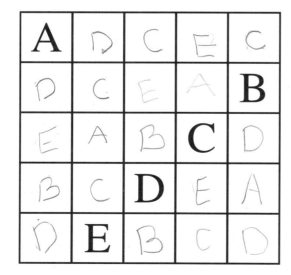

A	D	C	E	C
D	C	E	A	B
E	A	B	C	D
B	C	D	E	A
D	E	B	C	D

PUZZLE 3

You have accidentally left the plug out of the bath and are attempting to fill the bath with both taps full on. The hot tap takes 5 minutes to fill the bath and the cold tap 4 minutes, and the water empties through the plug-hole in 20 minutes.

In how many minutes will the bath be filled?

PUZZLE 4

How many circles appear below?

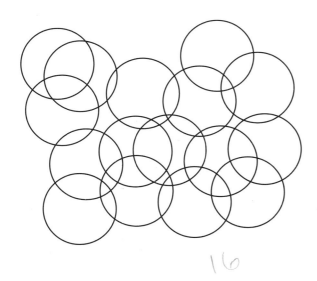

16

PUZZLE 5

What letter comes next?

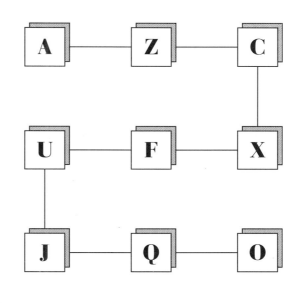

PUZZLE 6

7321 is to 143

and

8642 is to 3212

therefore

5126 is to ?

PUZZLE 7

Which number is the odd one out?

7426
6183
3248
9455
2573
8162

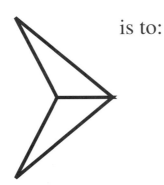 is to: 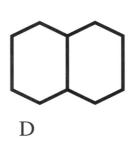 as: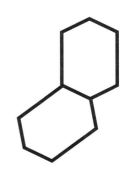

is to:

  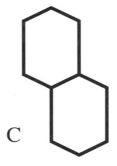 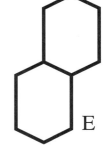

A   B   C   D   E

What number should replace the question mark?

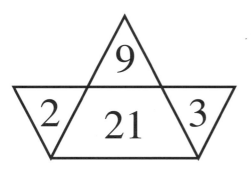

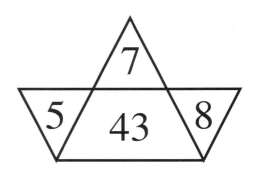

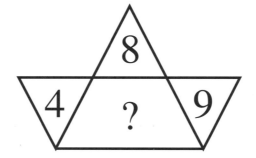

PUZZLE
10

When the left hand pattern is folded to form a cube, which 3 of the following can be produced?

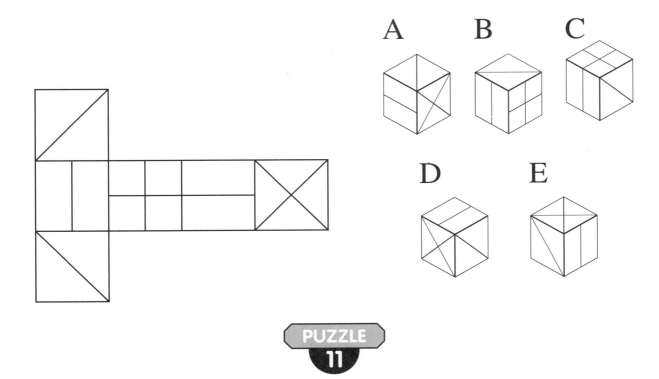

A   B   C

D   E

PUZZLE
11

Which circle would continue the sequence?

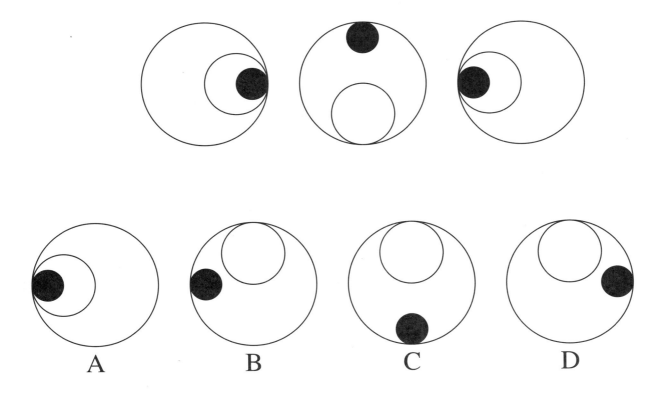

A   B   C   D

Each line and symbol which appears in the four outer circles, below, is transferred to the centre circle according to these rules: If a line or symbol occurs in the outer circles: once: it is transferred twice: it is possibly transferred   3 times: it is transferred   4 times: it is not transferred. Which of the circles A, B, C, D or E, should appear at the centre of the diagram, below?

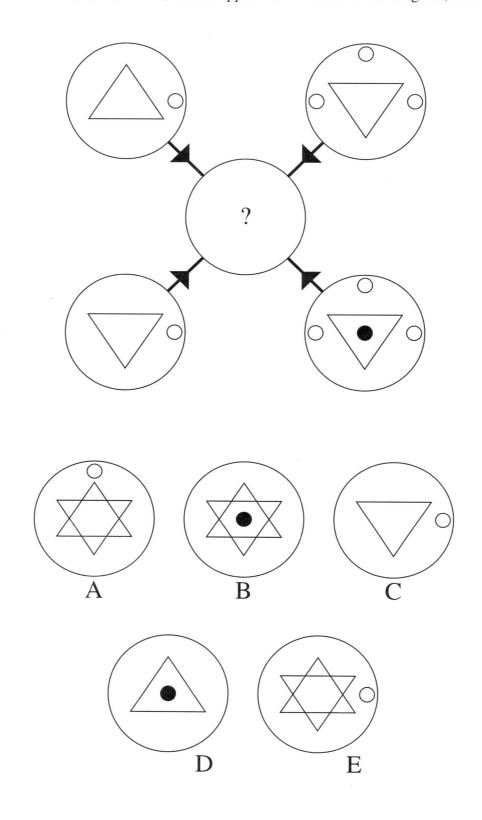

A

B

C

D

E

PUZZLE 13

What is the total of the numbers on the reverse side of these dice?

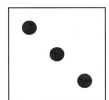 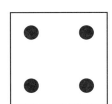 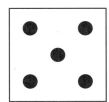 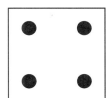 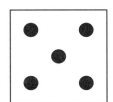

PUZZLE 14

Which number should replace the ?

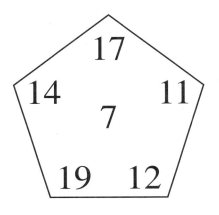 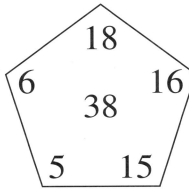 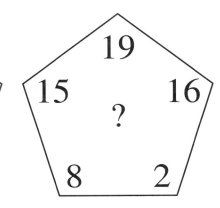

PUZZLE 15

Which word means the same or is closest in meaning to PASTICHE?

(a) ASSEMBLAGE
(b) ARTISTIC LICENCE
(c) NEEDLEWORK
(d) MEDLEY
(e) DEVOTION

PUZZLE 16

Which word means the same as NUGATORY?

SOUR
LISSOM
HARSH
FUTILE
KEEN
SWEET

S
E
C
T
I
O
N

2

23

PUZZLE 17

Which circle should replace the ? A, B, C, D or E?

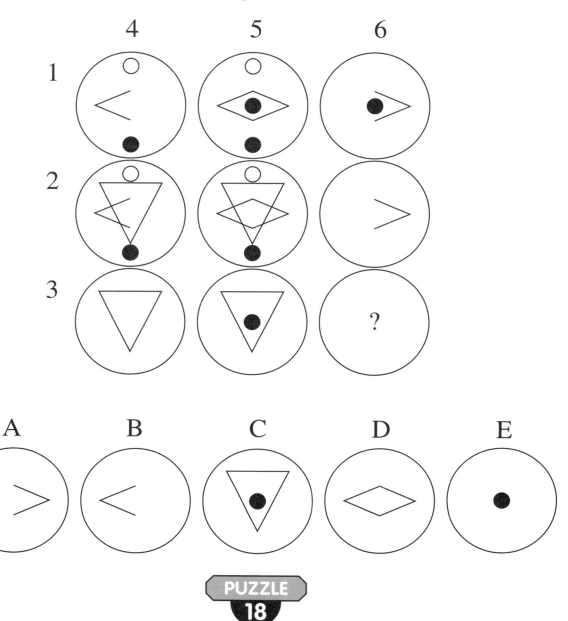

PUZZLE 18

Starting at midnight, snow fell 1 1/2 " every 6 hours. If there was already 2 1/4 " of snow at midnight, what was the thickness of the snow at 9 o/c ?

PUZZLE 19

Place a word in the brackets which means the same as the two words outside the brackets.

TAUNT (. . . . .) EAT GREEDILY

PUZZLE 20

Which is the odd one out?

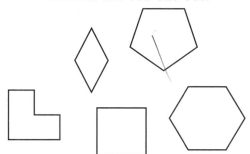

PUZZLE 21

Each of the nine squares in the grid marked A1 to C3, should incorporate all the lines and symbols which are shown in the squares of the same letter and number immediately above and to the left. For example, B2 should incorporate all the lines and symbols that are in 2 and B. One of the squares is incorrect. Which one is it?

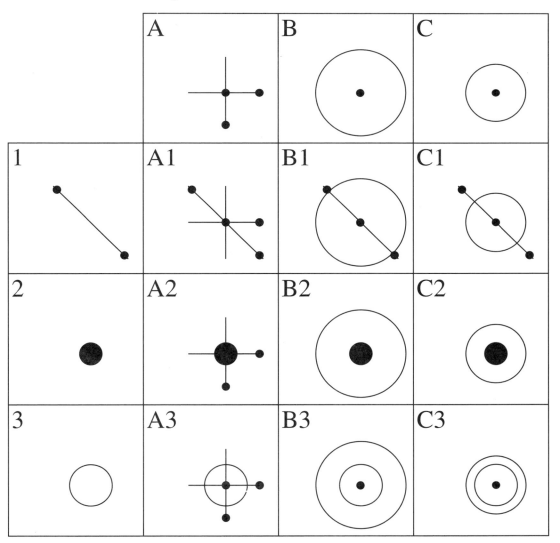

PUZZLE 22

Each symbol ♡ ♧ ◇ ♤ has a value.
Which symbol should replace the ? to make the
totals correct?

♡	♤	♧	♧	28
♡	◇	◇	◇	26
♡	♤	♤	♧	21
♡	♧	♧	?	32

44   15   22   26

PUZZLE 23

Simplify

$$\frac{9}{72} \div \frac{36}{144} \div \frac{12}{36}$$

PUZZLE 24

You have 13 diamond cards.

A 2 3 4 5 6 7 8 9 10 J Q K

What are the chances of drawing out K Q J 10 in that order?

PUZZLE 25

The answer is 12. Why?

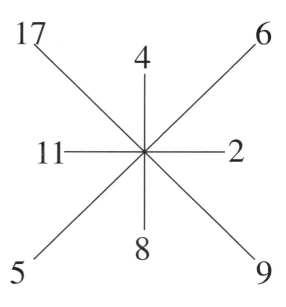

17   4   6
11   2
5   8   9

When the left hand pattern is folded to form a cube, which is the only one of the following that cannot be produced?

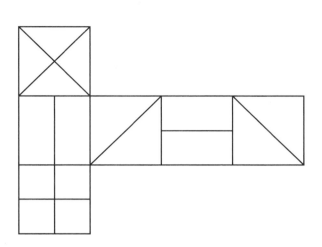

A   B   C

D   E

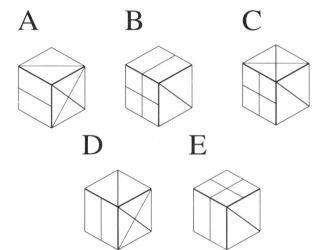

PUZZLE 2

What comes next in the sequence below?

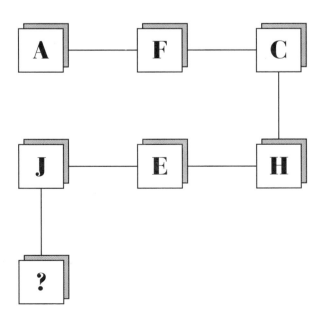

PUZZLE 3

What number is three places away from itself plus 3, two places away from itself multiplied by 4, three places away from itself less 2, two places away from itself plus 8 and three places away from itself less 1?

52	24	30	9	16
5	3	21	12	2
18	45	4	36	7
13	11	8	16	50
40	6	10	15	1

PUZZLE 4

You have a range of weights available from 1-10 units. They are all single weights. Which one should you use to balance the scale and where should you place it?

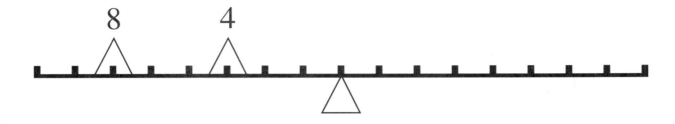

8   4

PUZZLE 5

Which is the odd one out?

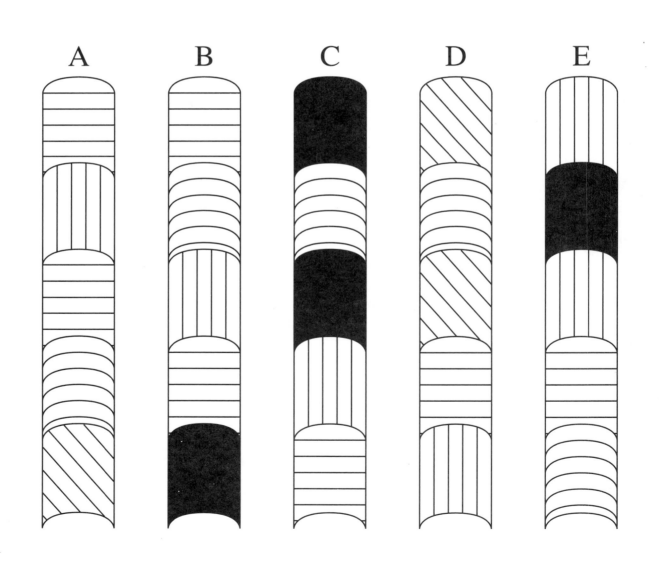

A   B   C   D   E

PUZZLE 6

In a game of 6 players lasting for 40 minutes, there are 4 reserves. They substitute each player, so that all players, including reserves, are on the pitch for the same length of time. How long is each player on the pitch?

PUZZLE 7

What comes next

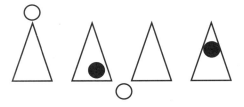

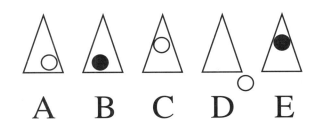

A   B   C   D   E

PUZZLE 8

What number should replace the question mark?

17	14	5	16
12			1
?			11
21	9	17	19

PUZZLE 9

What number should replace the question mark?

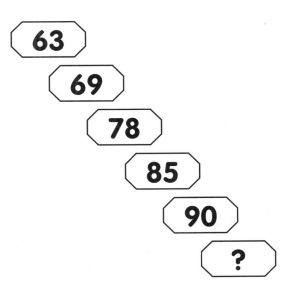

63
69
78
85
90
?

S E C T I O N

3

29

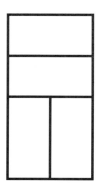 is to: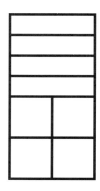

as:

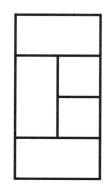

is to:

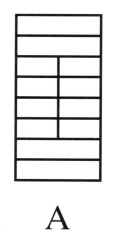

B

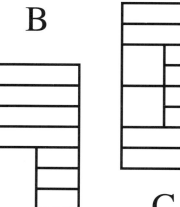

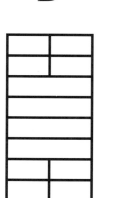

D

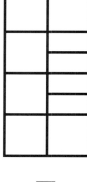

A

C

E

Which has the greatest total degrees in their angles, and by how much?

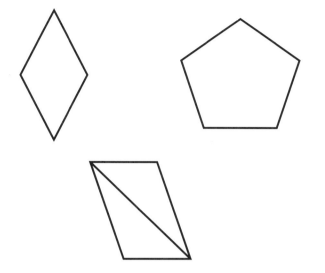

Find the value for A, B, C and D.

C	C	A	D	=22
C	D	D	A	=20
A	A	D	D	=32
C	B	B	A	=30

=24   =25   =23   =32

Which of these is not a musical instrument?

(a) CLARION
(b) PICCOLO
(c) CLAVECIN
(d) CANTAR
(e) OCARINA

Which numbers will replace the ?'s

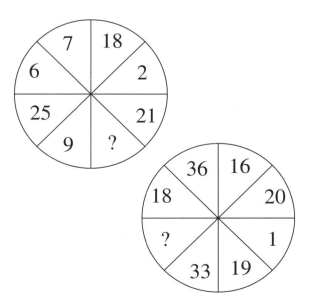

Each line and symbol which appears in the four outer circles, below, is transferred to the centre circle according to these rules: If a line or symbol occurs in the outer circles: once: it is transferred twice: it is possibly transferred   3 times: it is transferred   4 times: it is not transferred. Which of the circles A, B, C, D or E, should appear at the centre of the diagram, below?

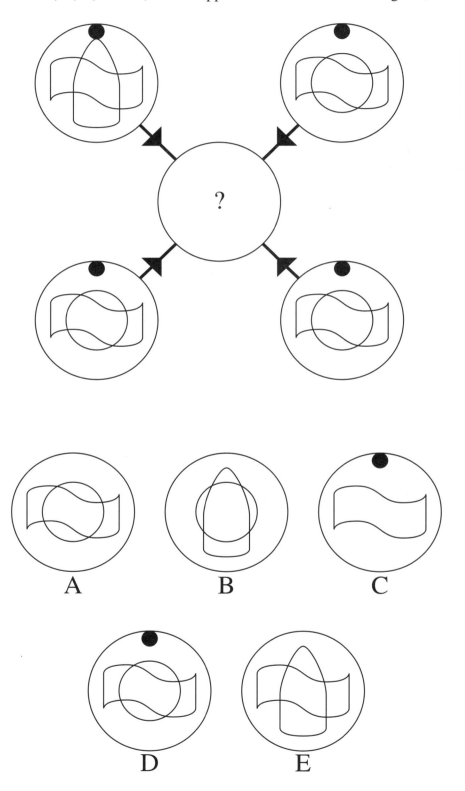

PUZZLE 16

What replaces the ?

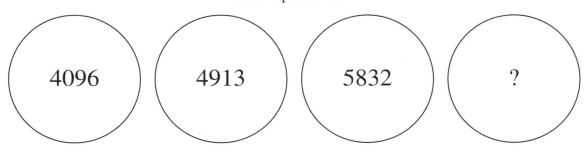

4096   4913   5832   ?

PUZZLE 17

What number should replace the ?

9
6
8 7   4 6
20
1   8
13   10

11
5
12 2   2 8
30
4   1
6   7

17
11
14 7   4 7
?
3   2
12   9

PUZZLE 18

The answer is 156, why?

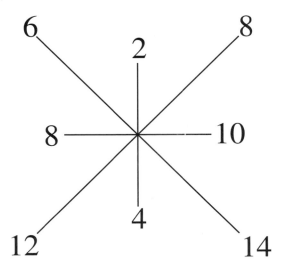

6   8
2
8 —————— 10
4
12   14

PUZZLE 19

Simplify

$(89^2) - (88^2)$

(a) 176

(b) 177

(c) 178

(d) 179

(e) 180

S
E
C
T
I
O
N

3

33

Which should replace the ? A, B, C or D?

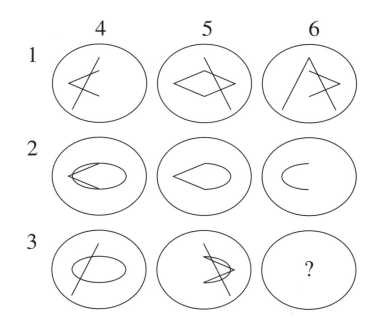

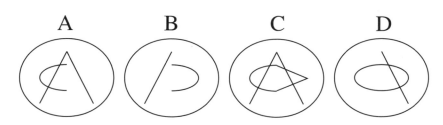

PUZZLE
21

PUZZLE
22

What number should go under the letter E?

Which word has the same or closest meaning to PALPABLE?

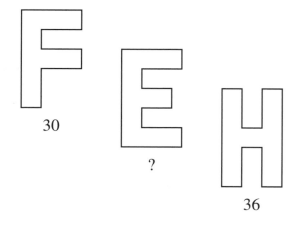

30

?

36

**(a) LIKENESS
(b) THROBBING
(c) CRUSHED
(d) CLEVER
(e) OBVIOUS**

Each of the nine squares in the grid marked A1 to C3, should incorporate all the lines and symbols which are shown in the squares of the same letter and number immediately above and to the left. For example, B2 should incorporate all the lines and symbols that are in 2 and B. One of the squares is incorrect. Which one is it?

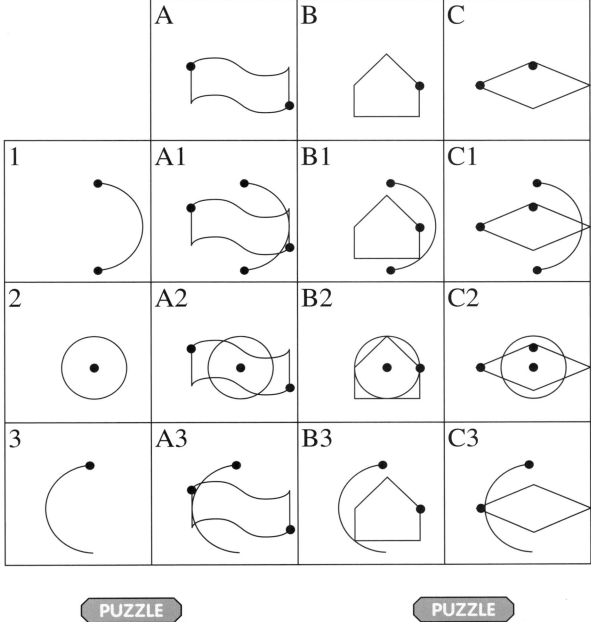

PUZZLE 24

The average of two numbers is 41 1/2
The average of three numbers is 72
What is the third number?

PUZZLE 25

The price of one pair of socks is $3.50
The price of a pack of 6 pairs is $19.50

What is the percentage cheaper when you buy a pack of 6?

SECTION

3

35

What heptagon below has most in common with the heptagon above?

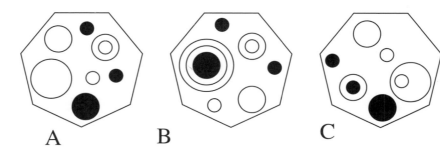

A   B   C

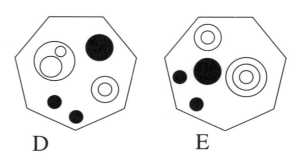

D   E

SUNDAY
MONDAY
TUESDAY
WEDNESDAY
THURSDAY
FRIDAY
SATURDAY

What day immediately follows the day three days before the day immediately before the day two days after the day immediately before Thursday?

What number should
replace the ?

1.5

4.5

13.5

16.5

?

PUZZLE 4

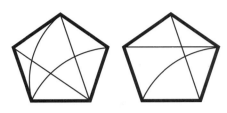   is to:

as:

is to:

A   B   C   D   E

PUZZLE 5

What number should replace the question marks?

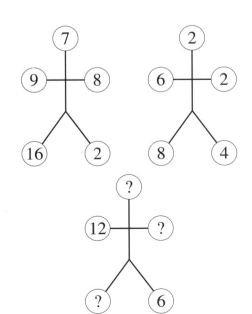

PUZZLE 6

A car travels 40 miles in the same time as another car travelling 20 mph faster covers 60 miles. How long does the journey take?

What should replace the circle with the question mark?

S
E
C
T
I
O
N

4

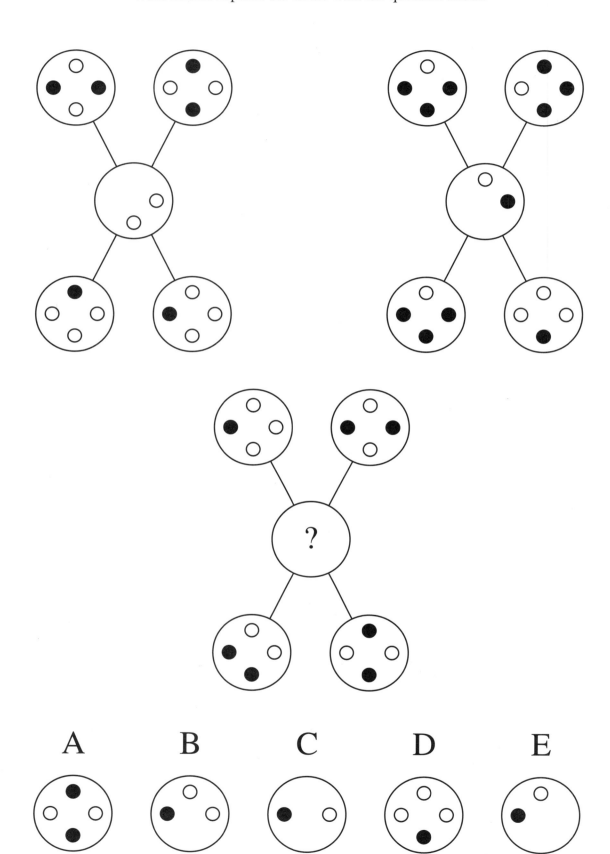

A   B   C   D   E

PUZZLE 8

What number should replace the question mark?

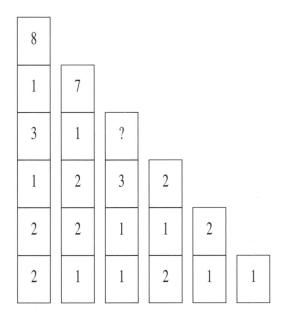

PUZZLE 9

All widgets are round. Everything round has a hole in the middle. Some things that are round have a handle. therefore,

1. All widgets have a hole in the middle

2. Everything with a handle is a widget

3. Neither of the above is true

4. Both the above are true

PUZZLE 10

Which is the missing tile?

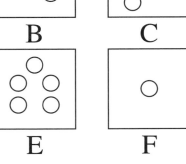

A   B   C

D   E   F

Each line and symbol which appears in the four outer circles, below, is transferred to the centre circle according to these rules: If a line or symbol occurs in the outer circles: once: it is transferred twice: it is possibly transferred 3 times: it is transferred 4 times: it is not transferred. Which of the circles A, B, C, D or E, should appear at the centre of the diagram, below?

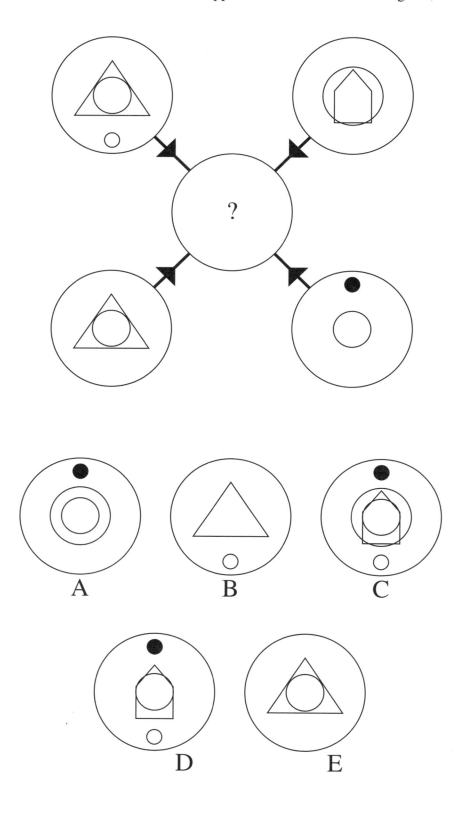

PUZZLE 12

Which letter should replace the ?

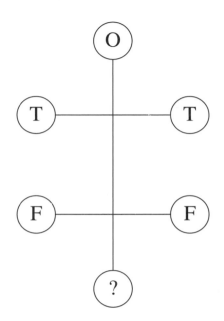

PUZZLE 13

Which is the odd one out?

(a) HESSIAN

(b) MARCASITE

(c) TAFFETA

(d) CORDUROY

(e) ORGANDIE

PUZZLE 14

Which words means the same as FETTER?

MANACLE,
BLANCHE,
SURPRISE,
LARGER,
SECONDARY,
STEAL

PUZZLE 15

Which is the odd one out?

A   B

C   D   E

F   G

PUZZLE 16

What should the time be on Clock D?

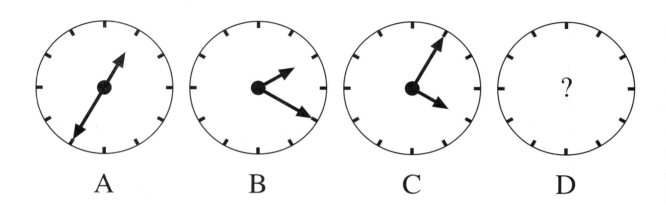

A   B   C   D

PUZZLE 17

What number should replace the ?

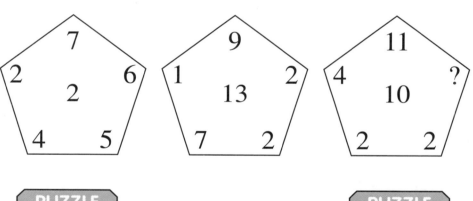

PUZZLE 18

PUZZLE 19

How many times must the large cog revolve before all of the cogs are in their original position?

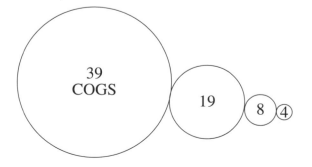

Which number should replace the ?

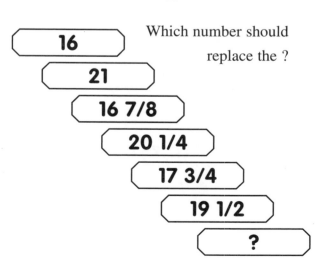

Each of the nine squares in the grid marked A1 to C3, should incorporate all the lines and symbols which are shown in the squares of the same letter and number immediately above and to the left. For example, B2 should incorporate all the lines and symbols that are in 2 and B. One of the squares is incorrect. Which one is it?

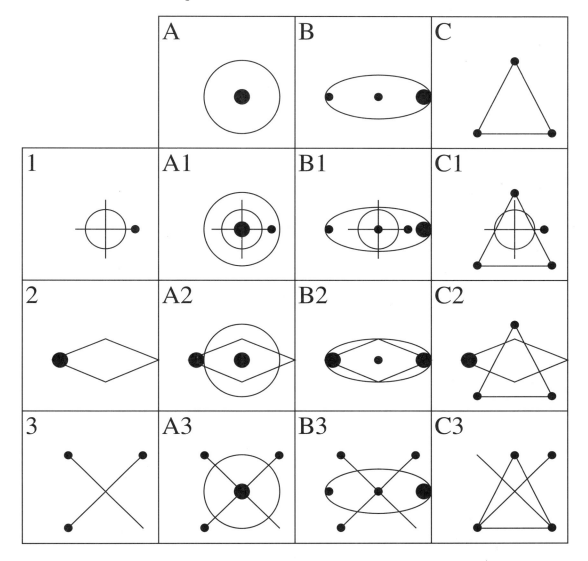

What is a PASHA?

(a) A DOG
(b) A TREE
(c) A TURKISH TITLE
(d) A DISH
(e) A BOAT

Which number comes next to a definite rule?

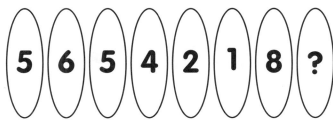

5 6 5 4 2 1 8 ?

S
E
C
T
I
O
N

4

PUZZLE
23

Which hexagon should replace the ?
A, B, C, D or E?

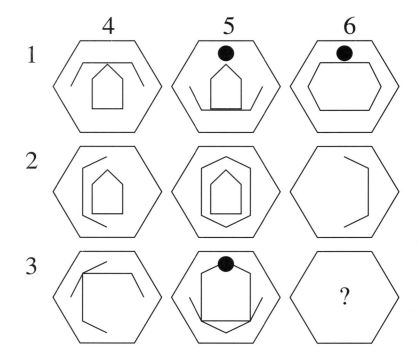

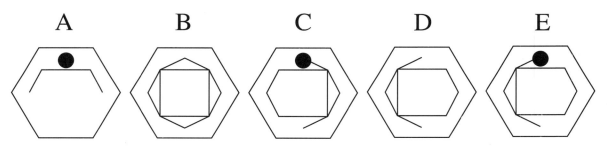

PUZZLE
24

PUZZLE
25

Which is the odd one out?

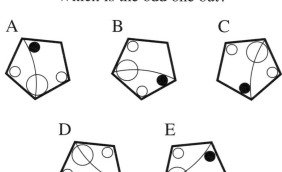

Simplify

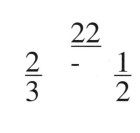

$$\frac{2}{3} \quad \overset{\underline{22}}{-} \quad \frac{1}{2}$$

PUZZLE 1

Which is the missing piece?

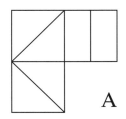 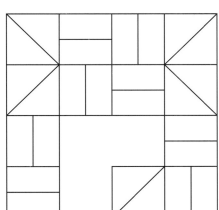 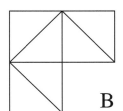

A

B

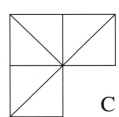 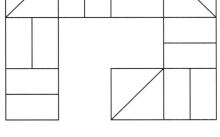 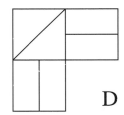

C

D

PUZZLE 2

E H L   is to   **VSO**

as

J K S   is to   **?**

PUZZLE 3

Which option on the right hand side
completes the set below?

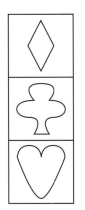 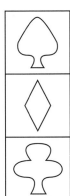 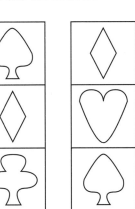 

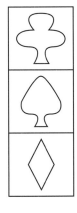 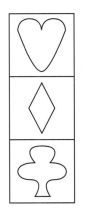 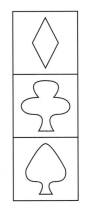 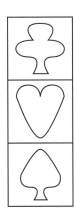

A   B   C   D

PUZZLE 4

What comes next?

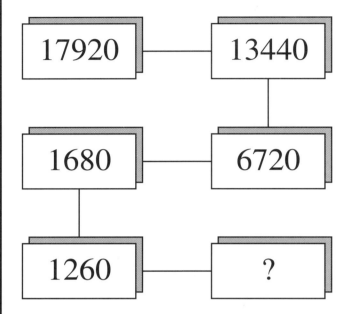

17920 — 13440

1680 — 6720

1260 — ?

PUZZLE 5

What number should replace the question mark?

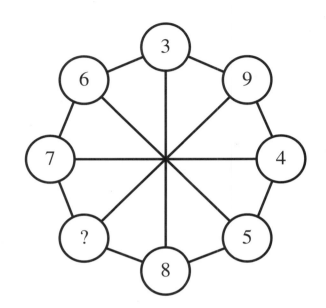

PUZZLE 6

What letter should replace the question mark?

T	
V	R
X	P
Z	N
B	?
D	J
F	H

PUZZLE 7

Which is the odd one out

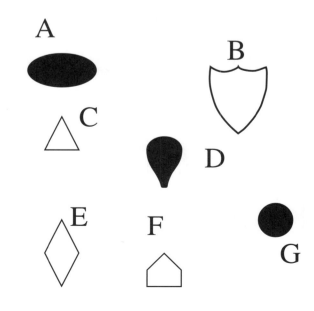

A
B
C
D
E
F
G

PUZZLE 8

What number should replace the question mark?

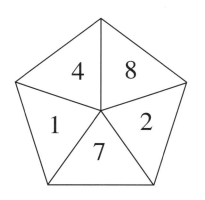

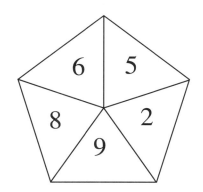

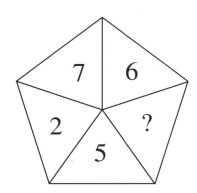

PUZZLE 9

Tanya can swim faster than Jack but slower than Sally. Harry usually swims faster than Jack, sometimes swims faster than Tanya, but never swims faster than Sally. Who is the slowest swimmer?

PUZZLE 10

What comes next?

A    B

C    D

E   F

Each line and symbol which appears in the four outer circles, below, is transferred to the centre circle according to these rules: If a line or symbol occurs in the outer circles: once: it is transferred twice: it is possibly transferred   3 times: it is transferred 4 times: it is not transferred. Which of the circles A, B, C, D or E, should appear at the centre of the diagram, below?

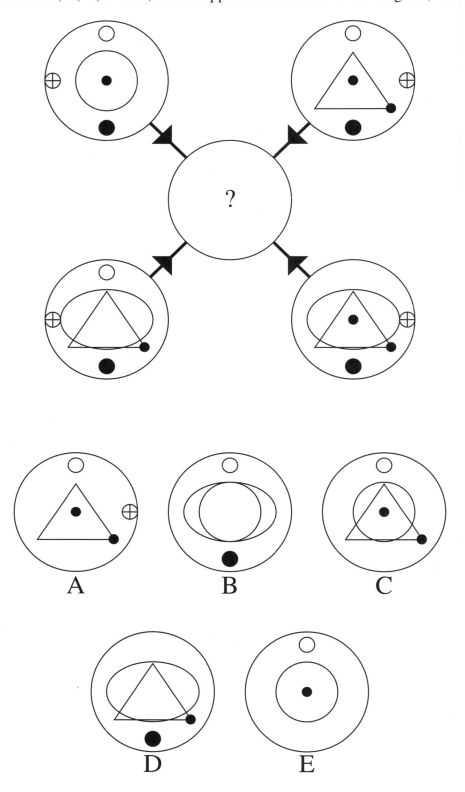

PUZZLE 12

What number should replace the ?

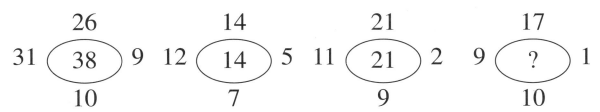

26		14		21		17	
31 (38) 9		12 (14) 5		11 (21) 2		9 (?) 1	
10		7		9		10	

PUZZLE 13

What number should replace the ?

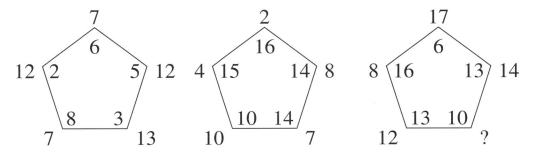

PUZZLE 14

Which hexagon A, B, C or D replaces the ?

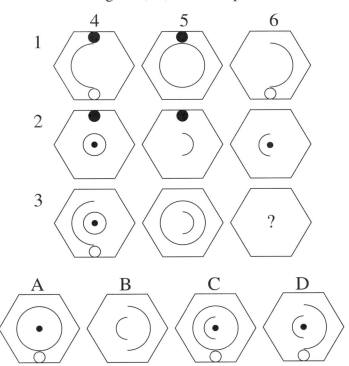

PUZZLE 15

Which circle should replace the ?

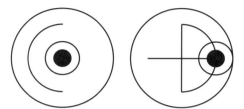

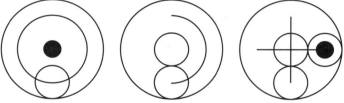

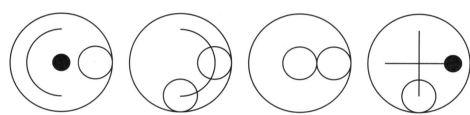

A   B   C   D   E

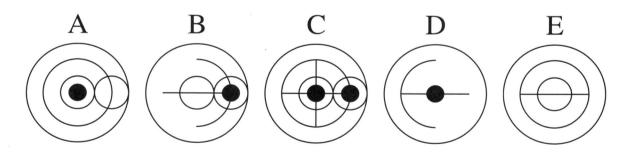

PUZZLE 16

Which word means the opposite of FASHIONABLE?

PIOUS, RETROUSSE, DENIGRATED, REPULSION, SANGUINE, DEMODED, FURBISHED

PUZZLE 17

Which is the odd one out?

PAVANE, ELANCE, FARANDOLE, GALLIARD, CHARLESTON

PUZZLE 18

Which of these is the odd one out?

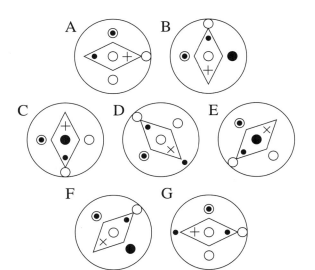

PUZZLE 19

How many revolutions must the largest cog make in order to bring the cogs back to their original positions?

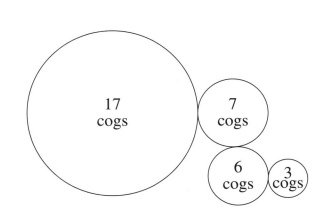

PUZZLE 20

if 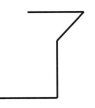 is to:

then  is to:

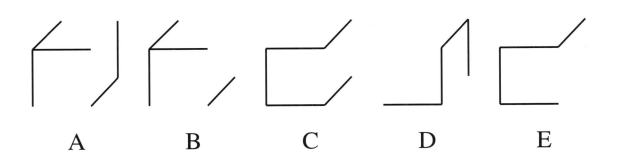

A   B   C   D   E

PUZZLE 21

What number should replace the ?

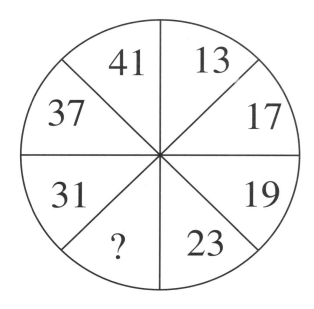

PUZZLE 22

What number should replace the ?

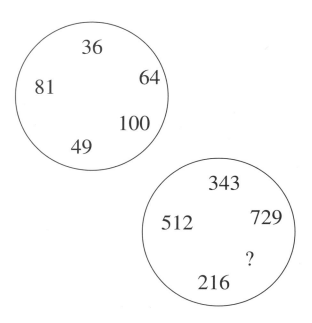

PUZZLE 23

What is a CHALDRON?

(a) A DISH

(b) A JEWEL

(c) A COAL MEASURE

(d) A MINERAL

(e) A CARD GAME

PUZZLE 24

Which of the following is always part of CANNELIONI?

(a) PASTA

(b) TRIPE

(c) HONEY

(d) BREAD

(e) ICE CREAM

What circle should replace the question mark?

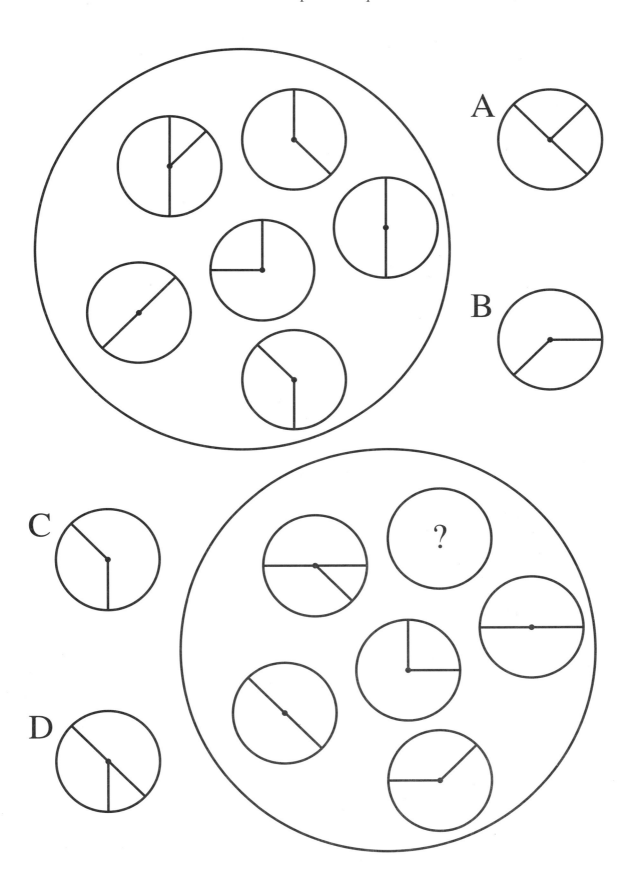

PUZZLE 1

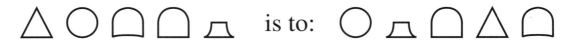 is to: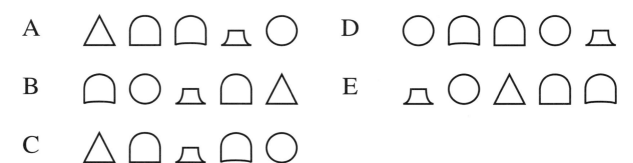

as:

is to:

A   D

B   E

C

PUZZLE 2

The die is rolled one face to square 2 and so on, one face at a time to squares 3 - 4 - 5- 6. Which number will appear on the top face in square 6?

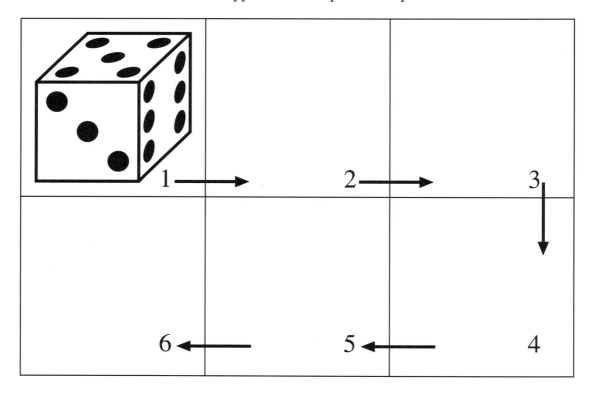

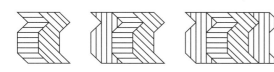

What comes next?

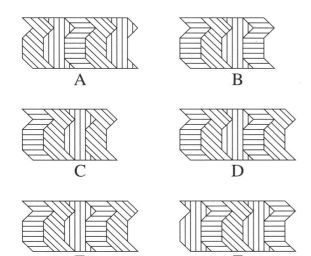

A B

C D

E F

Josie has £600 to spend. She spends 3/5 of the £600 on clothes, 0.45 of the remainder at a beauty salon and writes out a cheque for £150 for a new watch.

What is her financial situation at the end of the day?

What number should replace the question mark?

2	7
1	6

7	8
5	?

5	1
4	2

SECTION

What number should replace the question mark?

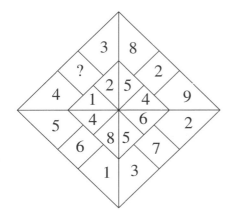

A C F H K M ?
What letter comes next?

What is the meaning of PANNIER?

(a) A GOLD MINER'S PAN
(b) A WOK
(c) A CLIMBING TOOL
(d) A BASKET

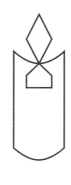

is to:

as: is to:

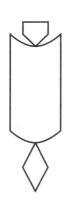

A   B   C

D   E   F

56

PUZZLE 10

What number should replace the question mark?

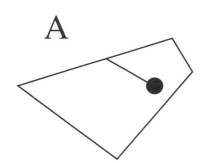

57

8 6

14 43

2 19

9 8

36 4 17 59 8 ?

PUZZLE 11

What comes next in the above sequence?

A

B

C

D

E

PUZZLE 12

Which is the odd one out?

A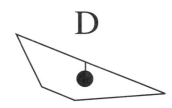

B

C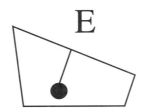

D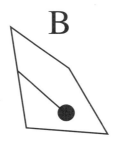

E

F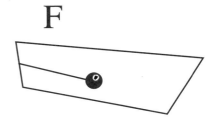

S
E
C
T
I
O
N

6

57

PUZZLE
13

Which is the odd one out?

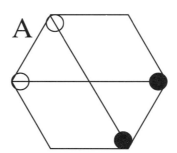

A

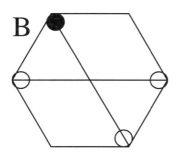

B

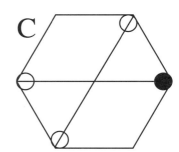

C

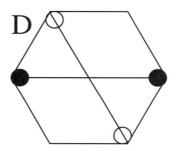

D

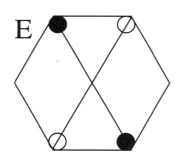

E

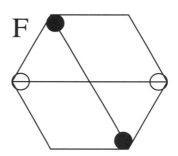

F

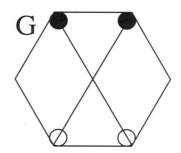

G

PUZZLE
14

What number should replace the ?

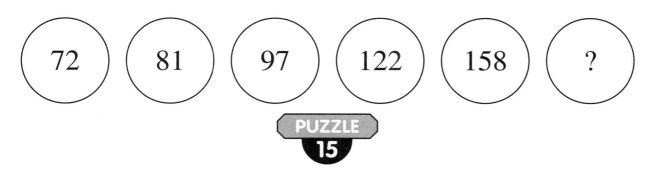

72   81   97   122   158   ?

PUZZLE
15

What number should replace the ?

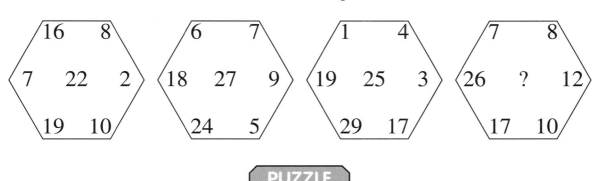

16   8   6   7   1   4   7   8
7 22 2   18 27 9   19 25 3   26 ? 12
19 10   24   5   29 17   17 10

PUZZLE
16

Which hexagon should replace the ? A, B, C, D or E?

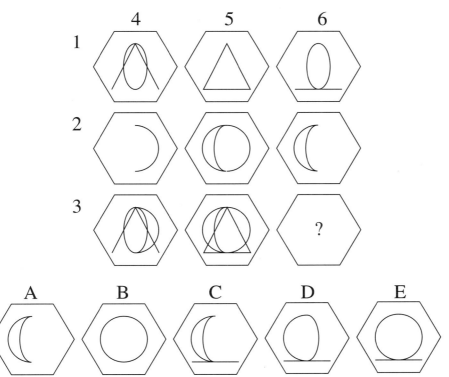

S E C T I O N 6

PUZZLE 17

Which is the odd one out?

(a) TIERCEL

(b) REEBOK

(c) LEVERET

(d) MEERKAT

(e) DROMEDARY

PUZZLE 18

1   2   3   4   5
                   ?

Choose the next shape from

A   B   C   D   E

PUZZLE 19

Which is the odd one out?

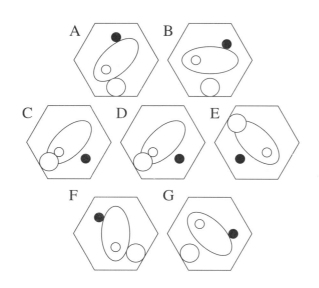

PUZZLE 20

Which is the odd one out?

(a) PAVANE

(b) MAZURKA

(c) RIGADOON

(d) CHARNECO

(e) FANDANGO

PUZZLE 21

If the temperature rises 15% from
x F to
103 1/2 F,

what was the previous temperature?

PUZZLE 22

What is a KNOUT?

(a) A KNOT
(b) A PLANT
(c) A PIG'S SNOUT
(d) A CLOAK
(e) A WHIP

PUZZLE 23

Which number should replace the ?

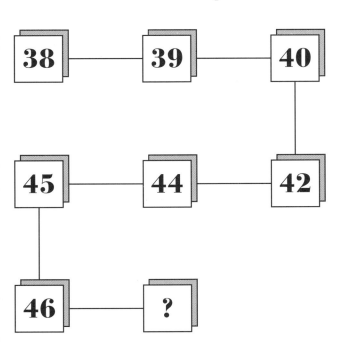

38	39	40
45	44	42
46	?	

PUZZLE 24

What weight should be placed at the ? in order to balance the scales?

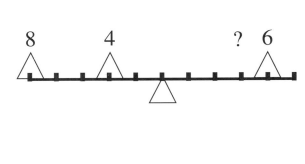

8   4   ? 6

S
E
C
T
I
O
N

6

Which circle should replace the ?

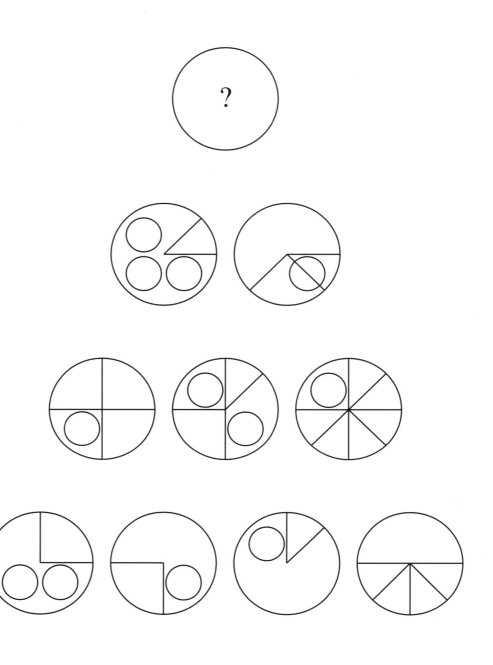

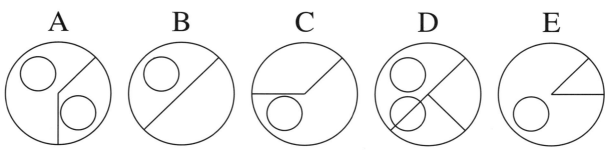

A   B   C   D   E

Which is the odd one out?

A

B

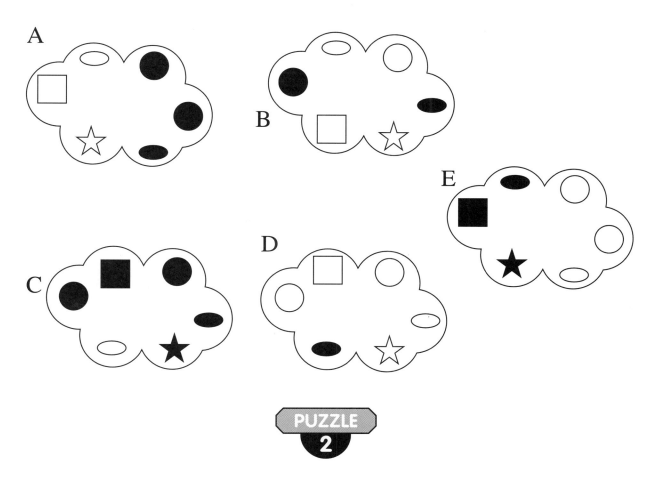

E

D

C

Insert the numbers into the circles so that the sum of all the numbers in the circles directly connected to each circle equals the total as given in the list below.

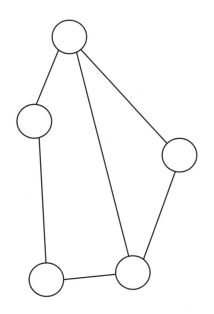

1=8
2=12
3=7
4=5
5=3

for example:

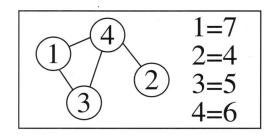

1=7
2=4
3=5
4=6

S
E
C
T
I
O
N

7

63

7

PUZZLE
3

Which is the odd one out?

A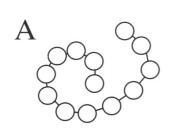

B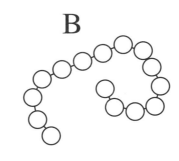

C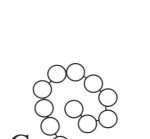

E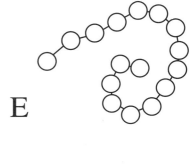

D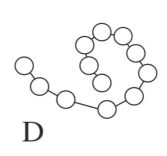

PUZZLE
4

Which set of letters is the odd one out?

KMOP
JLNO
GIKL
CEGH
SUWX
LMOP
OQST

PUZZLE
5

What number should replace the question mark?

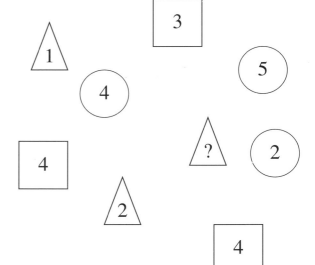

PUZZLE 6

Divide 600 by 1/4 and add 15. What is the answer?

PUZZLE 7

The cost of hiring a private rail carriage is shared equally by all the passengers who all paid an exact number of pounds which was less than £100. The carriage has seats for 50 passengers and the total bill amounts to £1887.
How many seats were not occupied?

PUZZLE 8

What number should replace the question mark?

1	3	3	5	?
0	2	2	4	?
2	1	4	3	?

PUZZLE 9

What comes next?

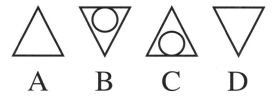

A   B   C   D

PUZZLE 10

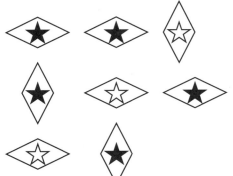

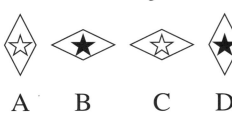

Which is the missing diamond?

A   B   C   D

PUZZLE 11

Which of these is the odd one out?

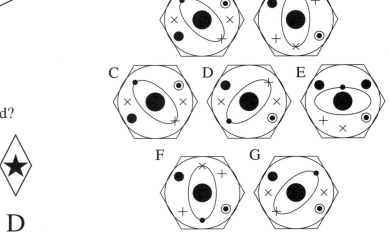

PUZZLE 12

What number should replace the ?

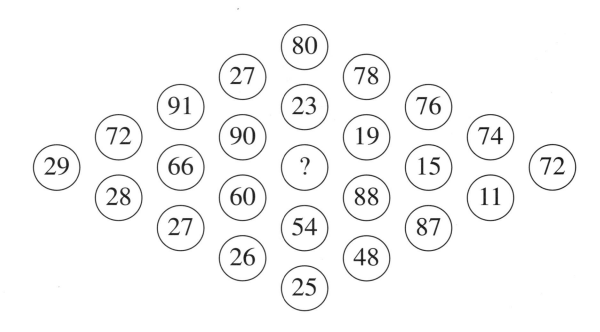

Each line and symbol which appears in the four outer circles, below, is transferred to the centre circle according to these rules: If a line or symbol occurs in the outer circles: once: it is transferred twice: it is possibly transferred 3 times: it is transferred 4 times: it is not transferred. Which of the circles A, B, C, D or E, should appear at the centre of the diagram, below?

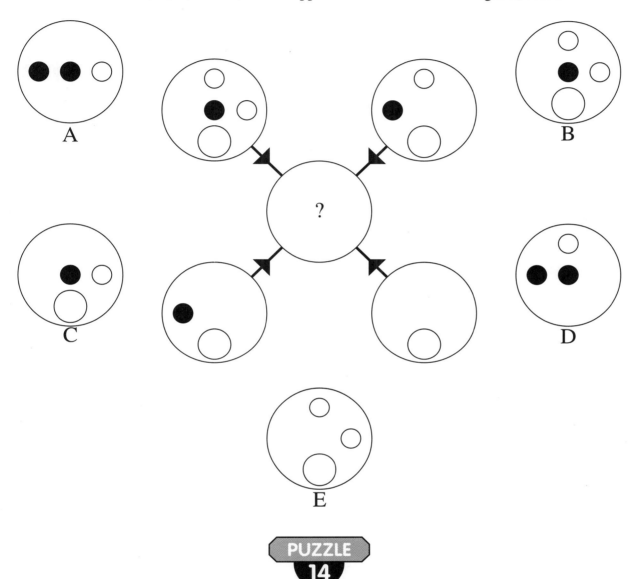

What number should replace the ?

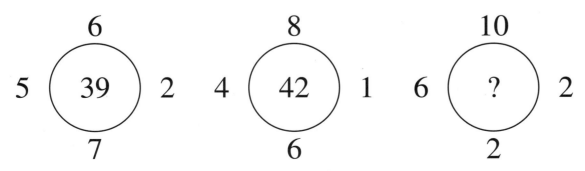

PUZZLE
15

Each of the nine squares in the grid marked A1 to C3, should incorporate all the lines and symbols which are shown in the squares of the same letter and number immediately above and to the left. For example, B2 should incorporate all the lines and symbols that are in 2 and B. One of the squares in incorrect. Which one is it?

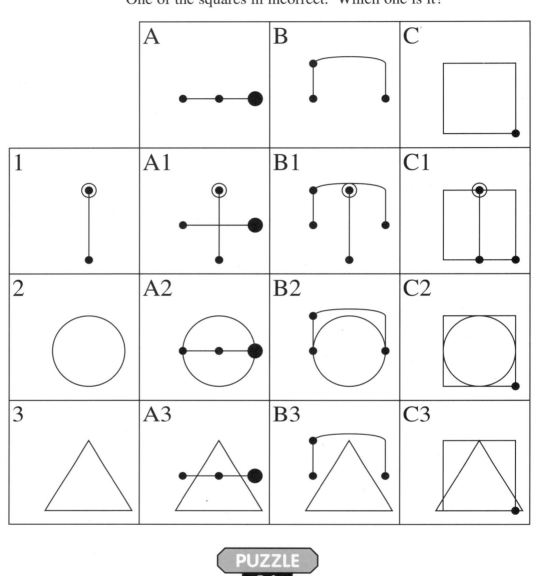

PUZZLE
16

What number should replace the ?

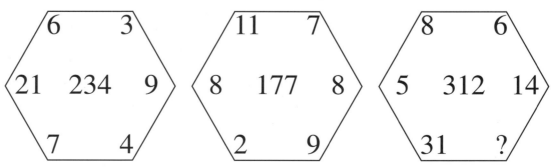

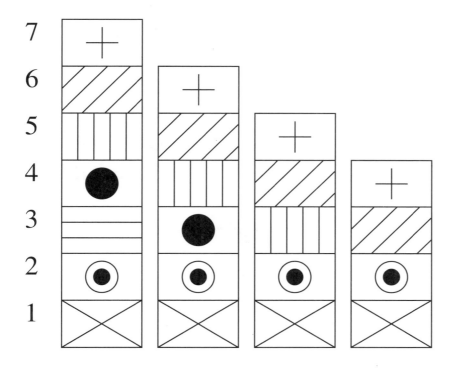

Which option below continues the above sequence?

A   B   C   D   E

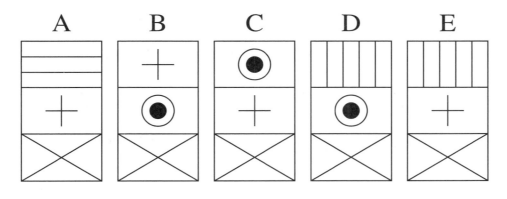

Which letter should replace the ?

A   H   L   T   ?

The combined ages of	are
ALAN + BERTIE	43
ALAN + CHARLIE	55
BERTIE + CHARLIE	66

How old are ALAN BERTIE + CHARLIE?

SECTION

7

7

PUZZLE 20

Which two words means the same?

PONIARD	-	CAUCUS
PITCH	-	PILLORY
SORREL	-	DAGGER
STAMEN	-	BLOSSOM

PUZZLE 21

Simplify

$$\frac{46}{27} \div \frac{92}{9} =$$

PUZZLE 22

At the dog show the dogs' numbers were

CORGI 11	-	TERRIER 15
WHIPPET 17	-	ALSATION ?

What was the alsation's number?

PUZZLE 23

How many KG should be placed at ? to balance the scale?

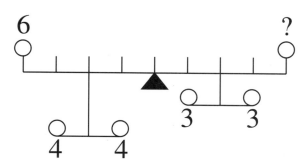

PUZZLE
24

A hundred eggs are in a crate, if you draw out 2, and there are 6 bad eggs in the crate, what are your chances of drawing out 2 bad eggs?

PUZZLE
25

At a school outing

81% of the boys had lost a shoe
82% of the boys had lost a sock
77% of the boys had lost a handkerchief
and
68% of the boys had lost a hat

What percentage at least must have lost all 4 items?

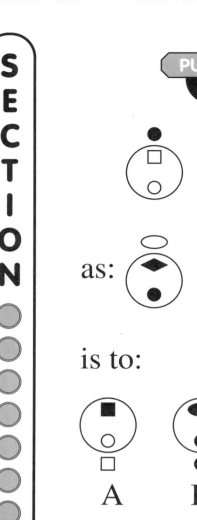

PUZZLE 1

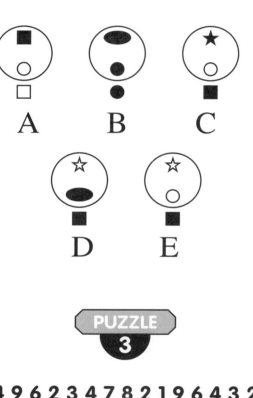

PUZZLE 2

What should replace the question marks?

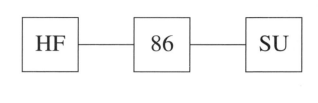

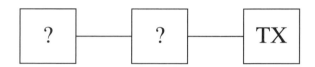

PUZZLE 3

4 9 6 2 3 4 7 8 2 1 9 6 4 3 2

Multiply by 7 the number of odd numbers which are immediately followed by an even number in the list above.

What is the answer?

PUZZLE 4

Which is the odd one out?

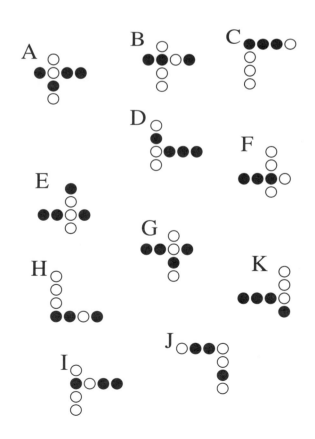

PUZZLE 5

Which is the missing shield?

A   B   C

SECTION

What comes next?

2
4
6
9
12
15
19
?

What number should replace the question mark?

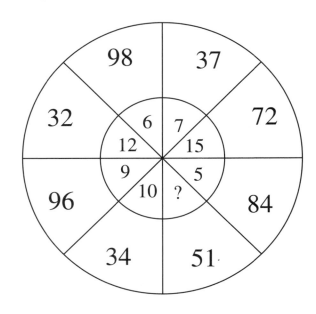

To which heptagon below can a dot be added so that both dots then meet the same conditions as in the heptagon above?

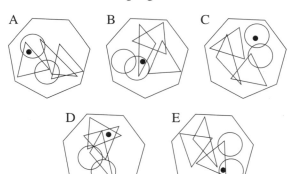

Find the starting point and visit each square once only to reach the treasure marked T.
1N 2W = 1 North, 2 West

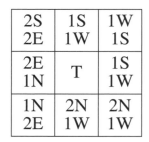

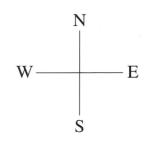

PUZZLE 6

PUZZLE 7

PUZZLE 8

PUZZLE 9

What comes next?

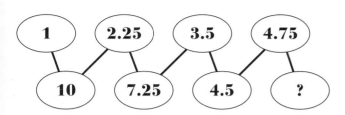

How many squares are there in this figure?

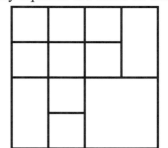

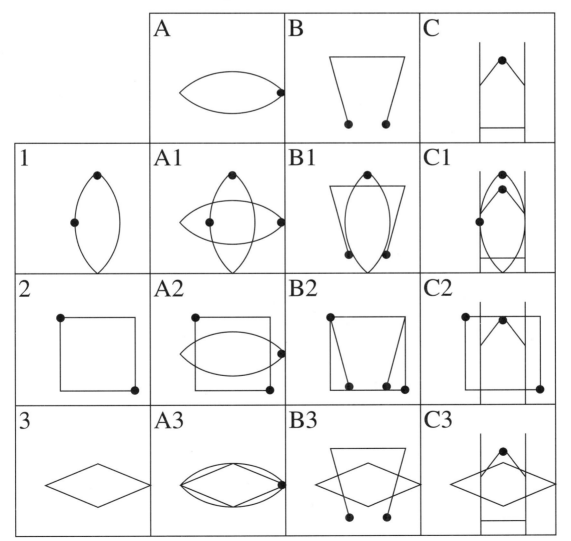

Each of the nine squares in the grid marked A1 to C3, should incorporate all the lines and symbols which are shown in the squares of the same letter and number immediately above and to the left. For example, B2 should incorporate all the lines and symbols that are in 2 and B. One of the squares is incorrect. Which one is it?

PUZZLE 13

What number should replace the ?

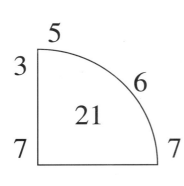

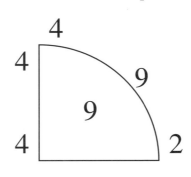

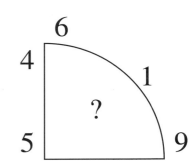

PUZZLE 14

What number should replace the ?

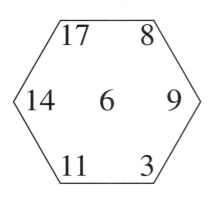

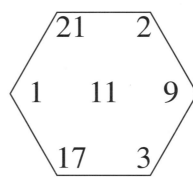

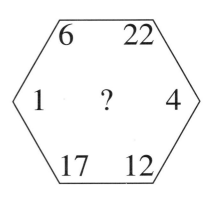

PUZZLE 15

What number should replace the ?

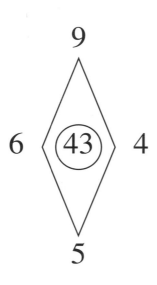

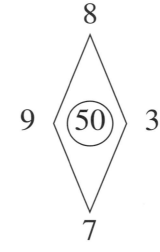

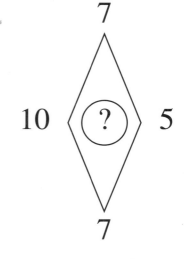

PUZZLE 16

Which square will fit in at ?

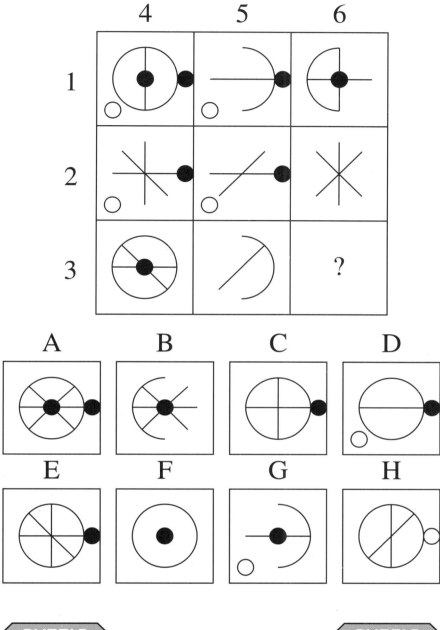

PUZZLE 17

PUZZLE 18

Find the weight to balance the scales.

6 KG   10 KG   12 KG   ?

There are two brothers and two sisters. In 10 years they will total 100 in their ages. How much will the total be in 7 years?

Each line and symbol which appears in the four outer circles, below, is transferred to the centre circle according to these rules: If a line or symbol occurs in the outer circles: once: it is transferred twice: it is possibly transferred   3 times: it is transferred 4 times: it is not transferred. Which of the circles A, B, C, D or E, should appear at the centre of the diagram, below?

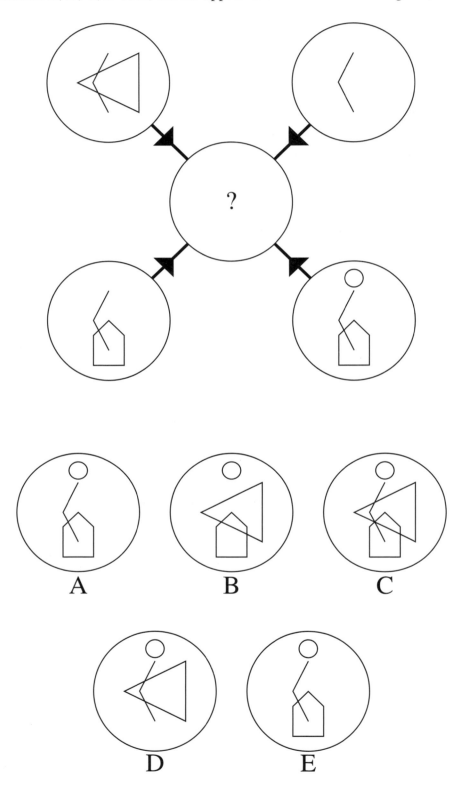

Which is the odd one out?

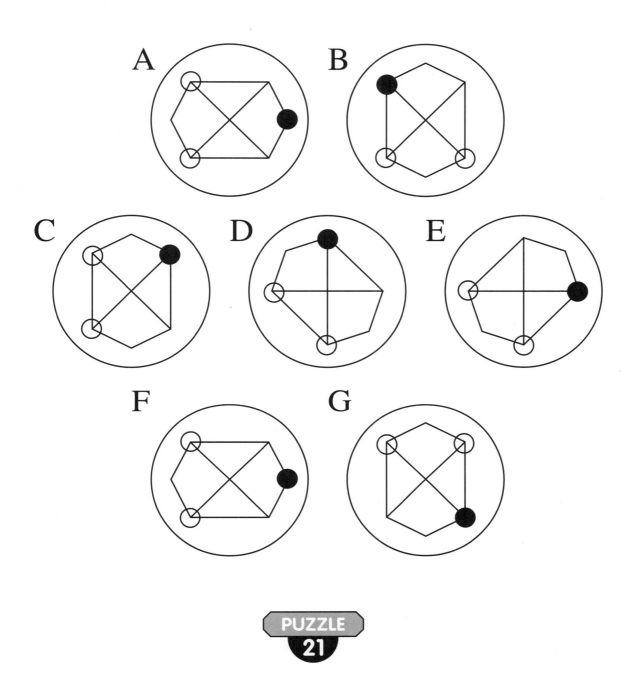

Insert the same number twice
(not the number 1) to make this calculation correct.

$$6 \div 6 = 6$$

PUZZLE 22

Which two words mean the opposite?

CORPULENT, DAZED, MERITORIOUS, VIRULENT, STANDARD, LEAN, UNCONCIOUS, END

PUZZLE 23

What number should replace x?

$$14 - (-7) - (-7) = x$$

PUZZLE 24

Out of 10 motors, 3 are defective. Two are chosen at random. What are the chances that both are defective?

PUZZLE 25

How many 4 card permutations (arrangements) can you make in a pack of 52 cards (standard playing cards)?

PUZZLE 1

Which is the missing piece?

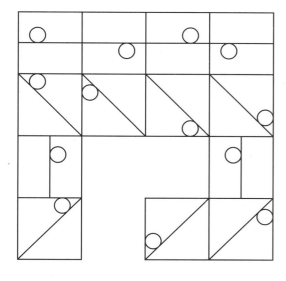

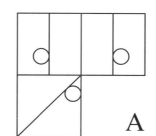

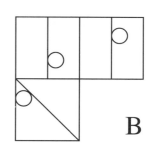

A

B

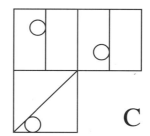

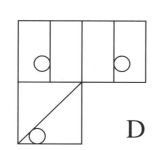

C

D

PUZZLE 2

Fill in the two missing numbers

5   36

4   ?   ?

3   57   78   93

2   15   42   36   57

1   34   19   61   25   82

PUZZLE 3

Which heptagon below has most in common with the heptagon above?

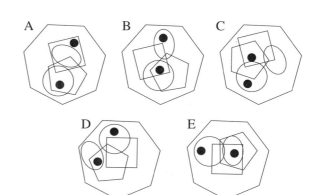

A   B   C

D   E

PUZZLE 4

A B C D E F G H

What letter is two letters to the left of the letter immediately to the right of the letter three letters to the left of the letter three letters to the right of the letter C?

PUZZLE 5

How many minutes is it before 12 noon if 132 minutes later it will be 3 times as many minutes before 3 pm?

PUZZLE 6

In how many circles does a dot appear?

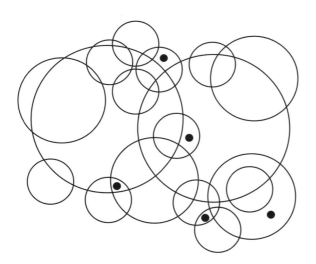

PUZZLE 7

What number should replace the question mark?

3			7			?	
2	1		1	1		1	6
7	8		3	9		9	7

PUZZLE 8

What is the value of the second line?

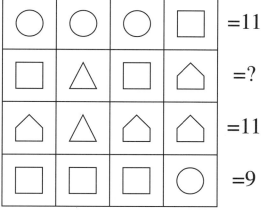

PUZZLE 9

What number should replace the question mark?

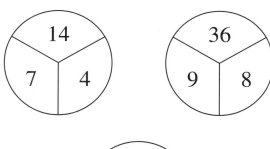
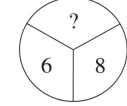

PUZZLE 10

How many lines appear below?

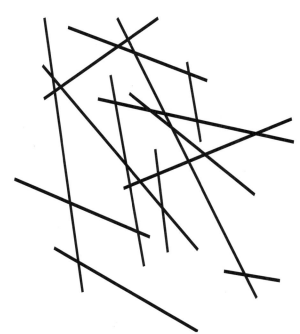

PUZZLE 11

How many triangles in this figure?

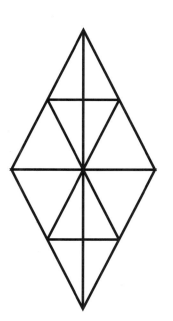

SECTION

9

83

Each line and symbol which appears in the four outer circles, below, is transferred to the centre circle according to these rules: If a line or symbol occurs in the outer circles: once: it is transferred twice: it is possibly transferred 3 times: it is transferred 4 times: it is not transferred. Which of the circles A, B, C, D or E, should appear at the centre of the diagram, below?

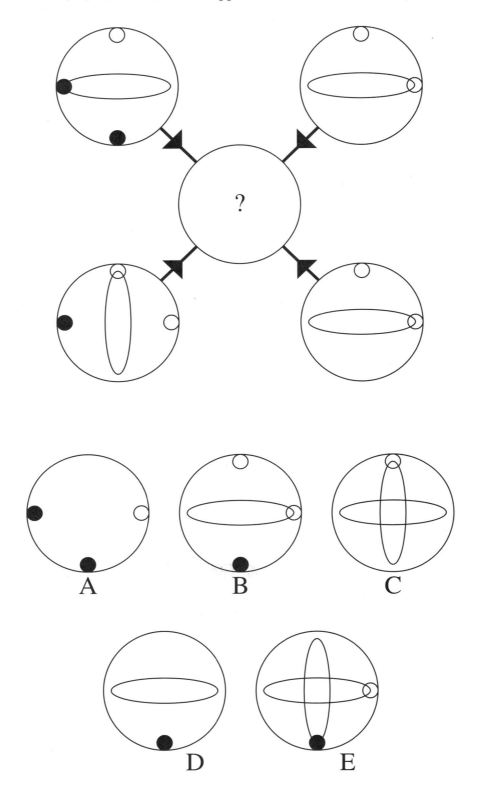

This grid consists of 3 squares marked A-B-C and 3 squares marked 1-2-3. The nine inner squares should incorporate the lines and symbols in the letter above and also the lines and symbols in the number to the left. One of the nine squares is incorrect. Which is it?

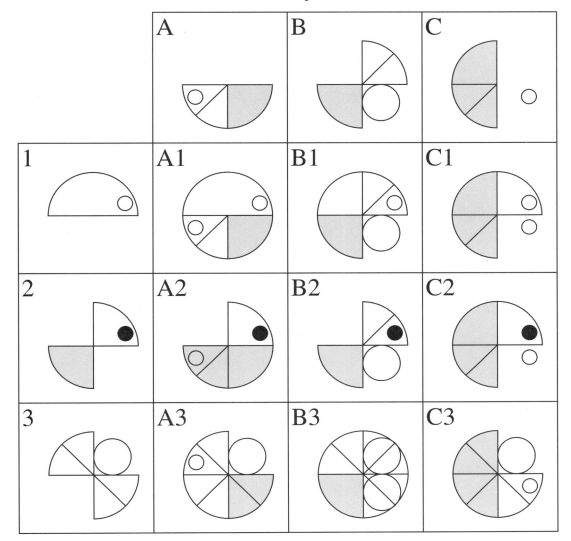

What number replaces the ?

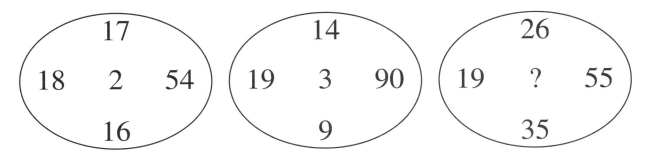

PUZZLE
15

Which hexagon A, B, C, D or E should replace the ?

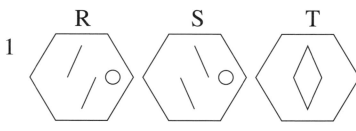

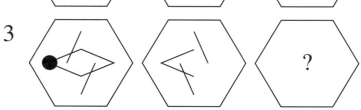

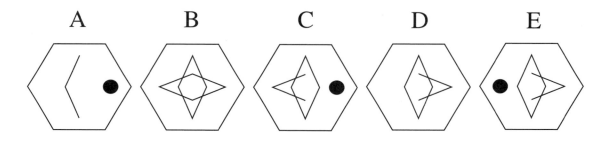

PUZZLE
16

What number should replace the ?

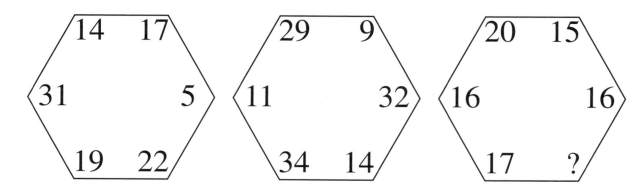

Which is the odd one out?

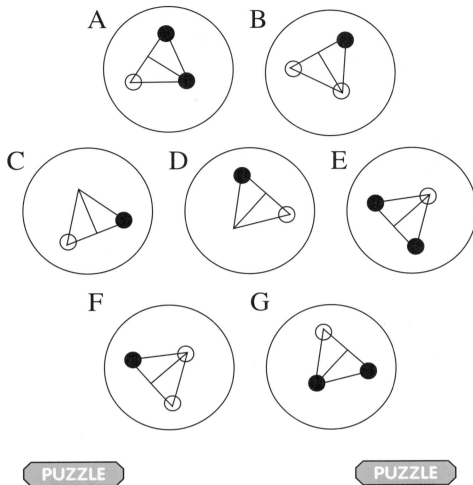

A B C D E F G

What number should replace the ?

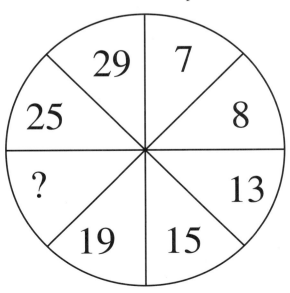

What number will replace the ?

17
41
20
35
23
29
26
?

PUZZLE 20

2 stations A and B have 4 stations between them. How many tickets must be issued so that a passenger can move from any station to another?

A   B

PUZZLE 21

How many different arrangements of the word LONDON can you make?

PUZZLE 22

Simplify and find the value for x.

$$3 \times 7 \times 14 - (8 - 5) - (12 \div 4) = X$$

PUZZLE 23

By which fraction does 19/36 exceed a 1/2 ?

PUZZLE 24

State Fair

At the eating contest the winner ate an average of 15 hot dogs at the first 20 sittings. After a further 20 sittings the average increased to 20 hot dogs. What was the average for the last 20 sittings?

PUZZLE 25

Which playing card should replace the ?

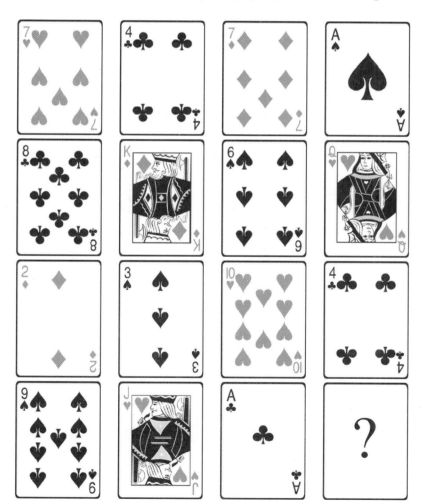

90

How many circles appear below?

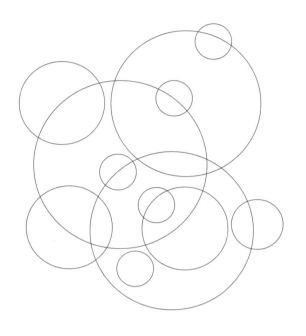

A train travelling at a speed of 80 mph enters a tunnel that is 0.5 miles long. The length of the train is 0.25 miles. How long does it take for all of the train to pass through the tunnel, from the moment the front enters, to the moment the rear emerges?

Which is the missing tile?

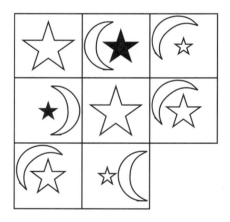

36 (36) 42

54 (25) 49

72 (?) 61

What number should replace the question mark?

A   B   C

D   E   F

PUZZLE 5

In a horse race, the first 5 places were filled by horses 4, 1, 3, 2 and 5 in that order. The jockey of horse 4 wore a green shirt, the jockey of horse 1 wore red, jockey 3 wore yellow and jockey 2 wore orange. Did jockey 5 wear purple, white, blue or black?

PUZZLE 6

A B C D E F G H

What letter is two letters after the letter immediately after the letter four letters before the letter two letters after the letter E?

PUZZLE 7

What is the missing tile?

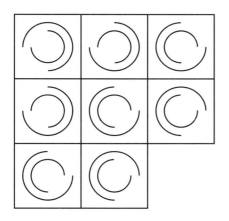

A

B

C

D

E

F

PUZZLE 8

What letter should replace the question mark?

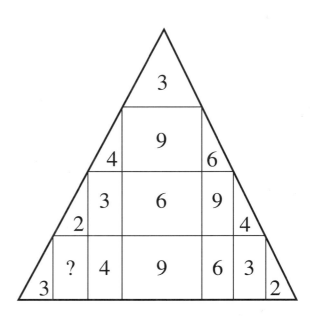

PUZZLE 9

What number is missing?

 **74286**

 28674

 67428

?

 **86742**

PUZZLE 10

What comes next?

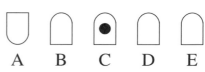

A   B   C   D   E

PUZZLE 11

What is the largest rectangle that can be cut from this piece of timber, in one piece?

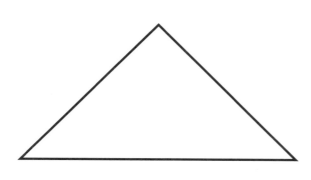

PUZZLE 12

There were 12 runners in the marathon. They lined up as follows.

8 5 4 46 52 61
7 6 9 94 63 ?

What number should the 12th runner have?

Each line and symbol which appears in the four outer circles, below, is transferred to the centre circle according to these rules. If a line or symbol occurs in the outer circles once, it is transferred; if it occurs twice, it is possibly transferred; three times, it is transferred; four times, it is not transferred. Which of the circles A, B, C, D or E, should appear at the centre of the diagram, below?

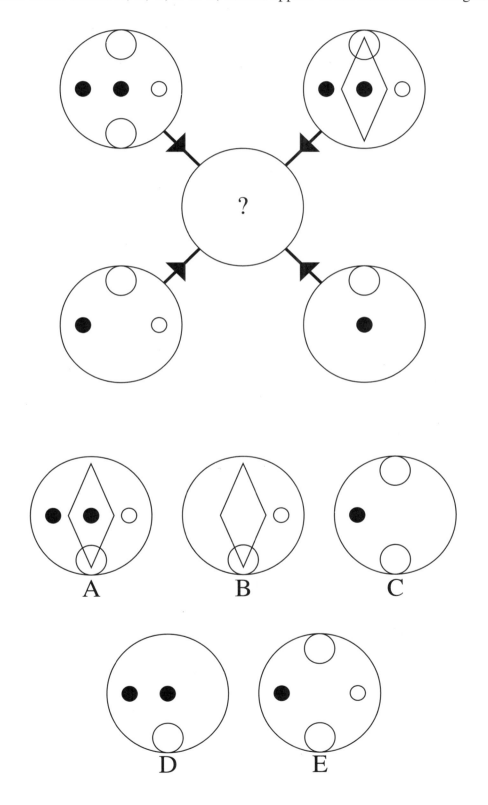

Each of the nine squares in the grid marked A1 to C3, should incorporate all the lines and symbols which are shown in the squares of the same letter and number immediately above and to the left. For example, B2 should incorporate all the lines and symbols that are in 2 and B. One of the squares is incorrect. Which one is it?

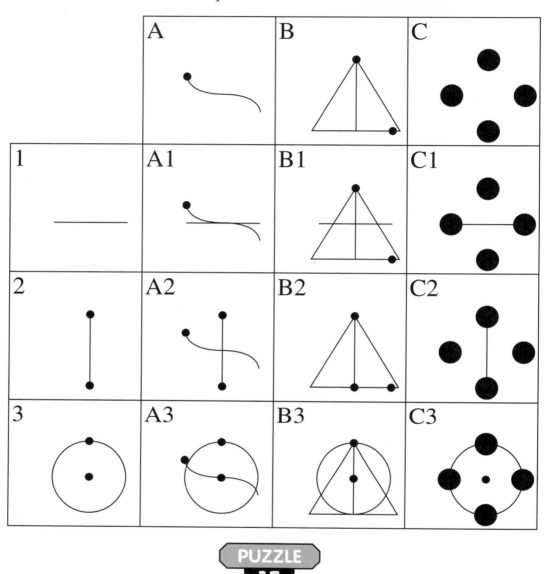

PUZZLE 15

What number should replace the ?

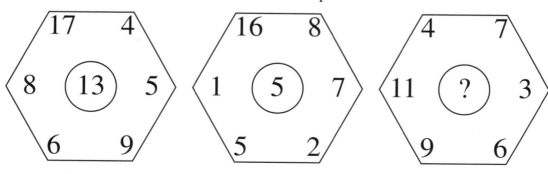

Which hexagon A, B, C, D or E should replace the ?

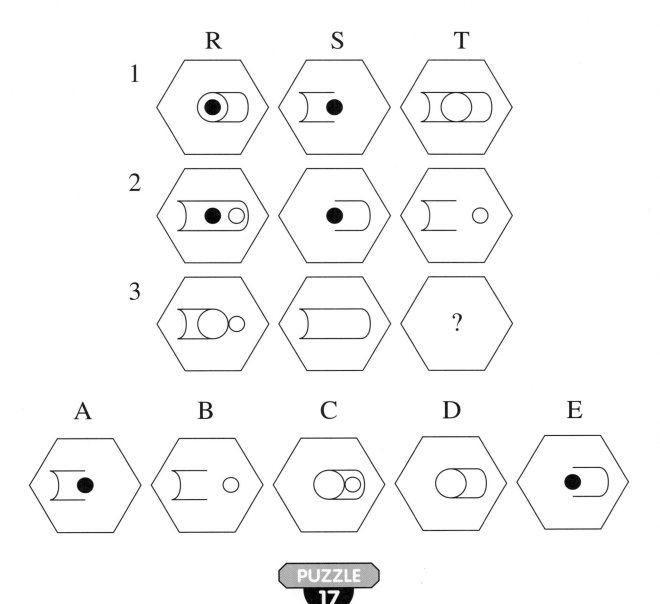

What number should replace the ?

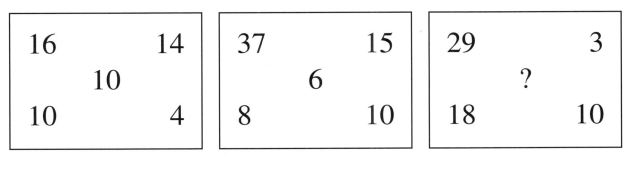

PUZZLE 18

I went into a furniture shop in order to buy a picture. The salesman told me - "The picture is five times the cost of that ashtray, the chair is 30 times the cost of the ashtray, the table is 4 times the cost of the chair, you can buy the lot for £312. What was the price of the picture?

PUZZLE 19

What number should replace the ?

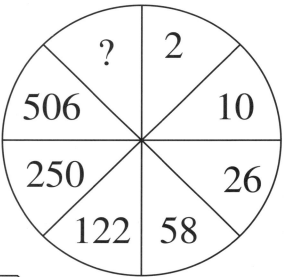

PUZZLE 20

Which is the odd one out?

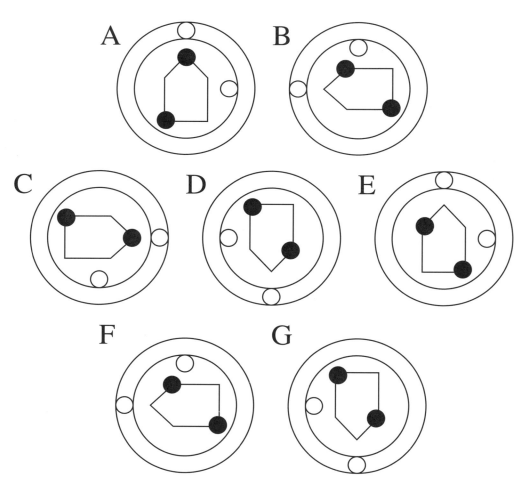

PUZZLE 21

How many squares are there on an 8x8 chess board?

PUZZLE 22

A school challenged a neighbouring school to a hockey match. The team to consist of 6 boys + 5 girls. The squad consisted of 8 boys +6 girls. How many different teams could they field?

PUZZLE 23

The invoice read "Wine" " - 67.9 - " The first and last digits were missing. There were 72 bottles. How much did each cost? (Each bottle cost the same).

PUZZLE 24

Three women, Mrs Black, Mrs Red, Mrs Brown, met in the hairdresser's. One of them said, "I have black hair and you two have red hair and brown hair, but none of us has the hair colour that matches her name."
Mrs Brown responded,"You are quite right."
What colour is Mrs Red's hair?"

Which playing card should replace the ?

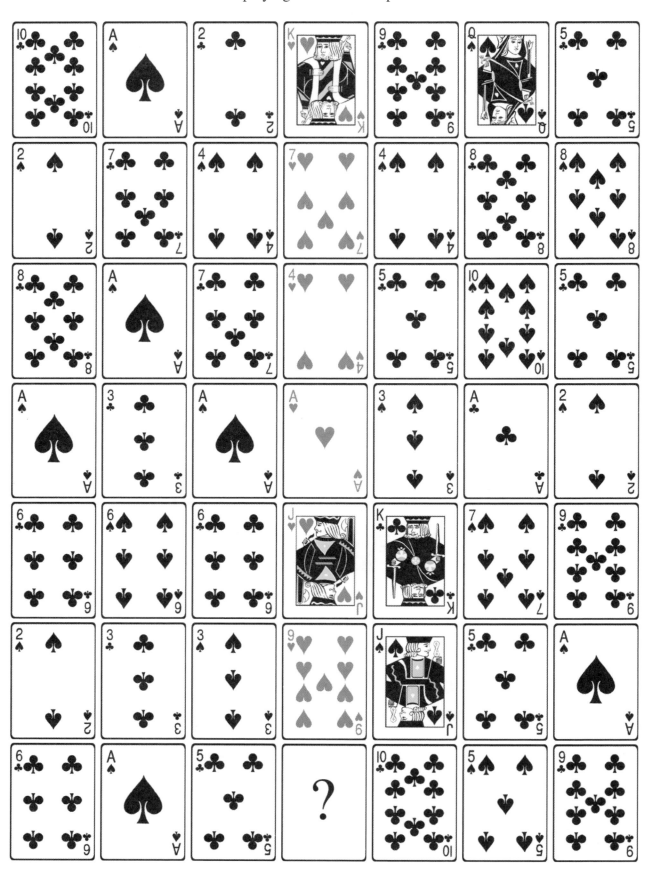

is to:

as:

is to:

A

B

C

D

E

PUZZLE 2

What should replace the question marks?

A	5	D	11	G	17	J
						23
7						M
?	?	Y	47	V	41	S	34	P	29

PUZZLE 3

What numbers should replace the question marks?

21	23	22	25	27	26
34	35	33	30	31	29
37	39	38	?	43	42
50	51	49	?	47	45
53	55	54	57	59	58
66	67	65	62	63	61

PUZZLE 4

Which is the odd one out?

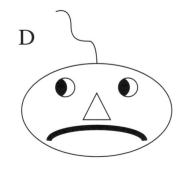

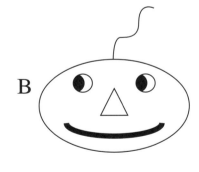

A

B

C

D

E

What letters should replace the question marks?

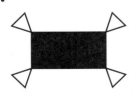

Diamond grid:
```
      F J
     L M T
    F J T M
  M T J F L
 L F J T M L
 F L M ? J F
  J T ? ? F
   L M T J
    F J T
     L M
```

2748 is to **414816**

as

3295 is to **641810**

therefore

6342 is to **?**

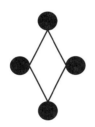 is to:

as: is to:

 A B C D

 E F G H

S
E
C
T
I
O
N

11

PUZZLE 8

Find the starting square and follow the directions to arrive on the square marked T. Every square must be visited once only.

1N, 3E means 1 North, 3 East.

2S 2E	2E 3S	2W 1S	3W
3E 1S	1E 2S	1W 2S	2S 3W
2N 3E	1N 2E	T	3W
1E 2N	1E 3N	1W 3N	2N 1W

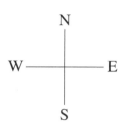

PUZZLE 9

What comes next?

A   B   C   D   E   F

PUZZLE 10

Insert the numbers 1-5 in the circles so that the sum of all the numbers directly connected to each circle equals the sum as indicated in the table shown.

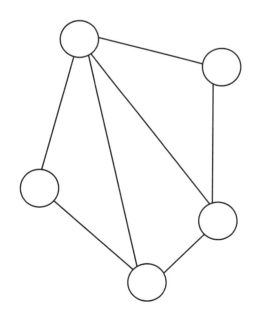

1=11
2=5
3=9
4=11
5=8

for example:

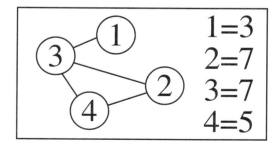

1=3
2=7
3=7
4=5

PUZZLE 11

Each line and symbol which appears in the four outer circles, below, is transferred to the centre circle according to these rules: If a line or symbol occurs in the outer circles: once: it is transferred twice: it is possibly transferred 3 times: it is transferred 4 times: it is not transferred. Which of the circles A, B, C, D or E, should appear at the centre of the diagram, below?

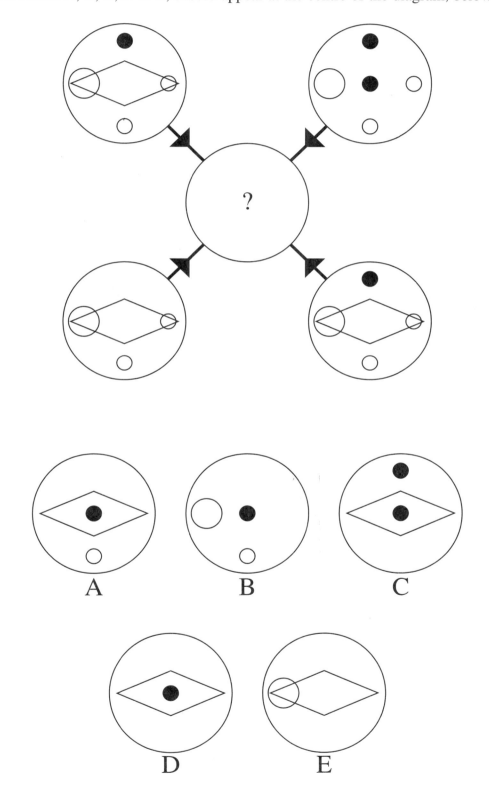

PUZZLE 12

Each of the nine squares in the grid marked A1 to C3, should incorporate all the lines and symbols which are shown in the squares of the same letter and number immediately above and to the left. For example, B2 should incorporate all the lines and symbols that are in 2 and B. One of the squares is incorrect. Which one is it?

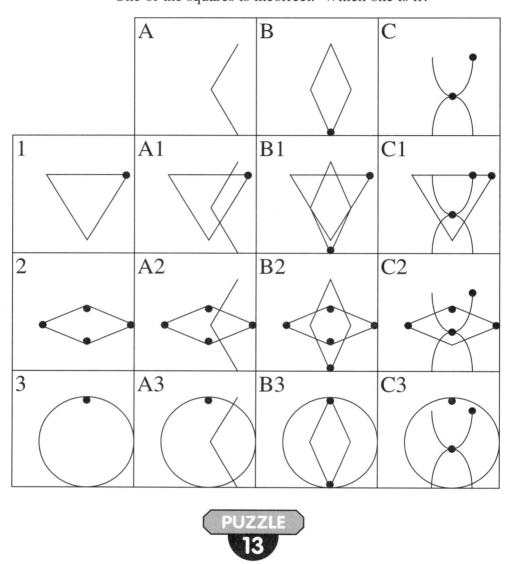

PUZZLE 13

What number should replace the ?

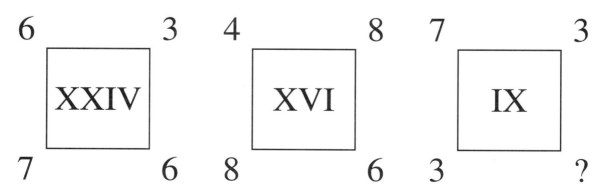

Simplify

$$\frac{7}{11} \div \frac{14}{22} \div \frac{20}{28} = \mathsf{X}$$

Which is the odd one out?

38   65   56   19   74   47   92

What number should replace the ?

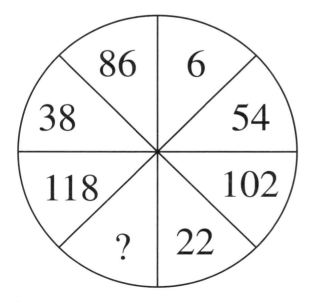

Which is the odd one out?

54   72   42   60   87   16   93

S E C T I O N

11

105

PUZZLE
18

What number should replace the ?

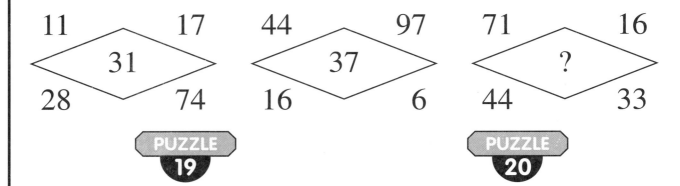

11   17   44   97   71   16

31   37   ?

28   74   16   6   44   33

PUZZLE
19

Which is the odd one out?

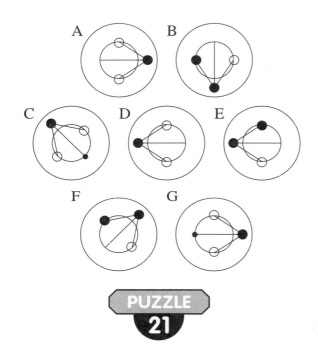

A   B

C   D   E

F   G

PUZZLE
20

An aircraft flew from A to B at an average speed of 230 m.p.h. It returned from B to A at an average speed of 300 m.p.h. What was its average speed for the two journeys?

PUZZLE
21

There are 12 trees in the orchard, can you connect them with only 5 straight lines?

:   :   :   :

PUZZLE
22

Replace the letters with numbers, so that the sum is correct.

WHAT
× A
SHOW

In a lottery of 6 winning numbers, how many tickets are there that include every set of 6 numbers out of 30?

A man left a sum of money to his 4 children. Bert received 50% of Cyril's amount. Alan received as much as Bert and John. Cyril received 125% of John's amount. John received £840. How much more did Alan receive than Cyril?

Which hexagon should replace the ?

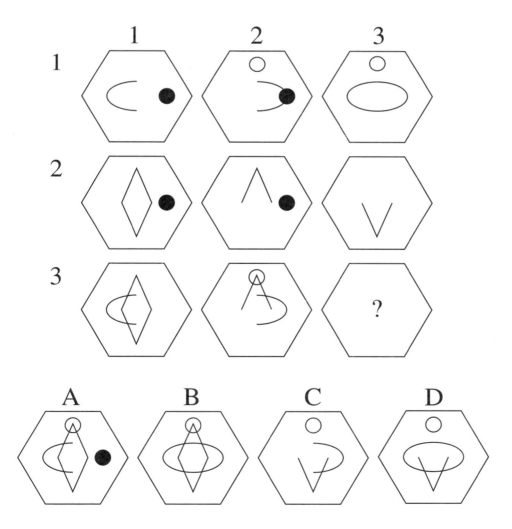

PUZZLE 1

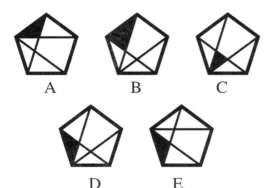

What comes next?

A   B   C

D   E

 PUZZLE 2

72 (158) 84

33 (126) 92

97 (?) 31

What number is missing?

PUZZLE 3

When the pattern below is folded to form a cube,
which is the only one of the following that can be produced?

A   B   C

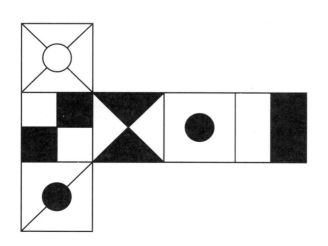

D   E

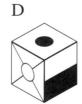 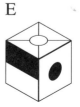

PUZZLE 4

A D F

is to

Z W U

as

G J L

is to

?

PUZZLE 5

Tom and Jerry share out a certain sum of money in the ratio 5 : 4 respectively, and Tom ends up with £275. How much money was shared out?

PUZZLE 6

When the pattern below is folded to form a cube, which is the only one of the following that can be produced?

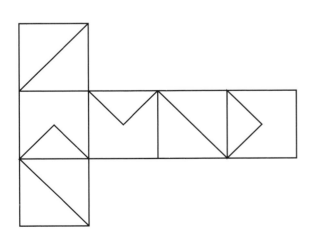

A  B 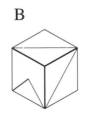 C

D  E

PUZZLE 7

What is the missing number?

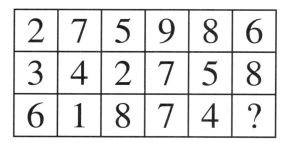

2	7	5	9	8	6
3	4	2	7	5	8
6	1	8	7	4	?

PUZZLE 8

What letters should replace the question mark?

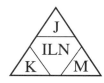

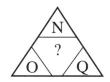

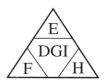

PUZZLE 9

Insert the numbers 1-6 in the circles so that the sum of all the numbers directly connected to each circle equals the sum as indicated in the table shown.

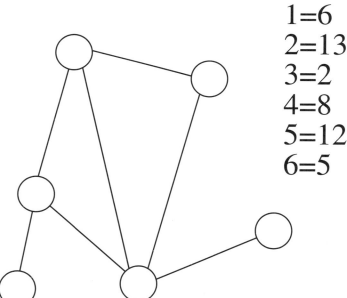

1=6
2=13
3=2
4=8
5=12
6=5

for example:

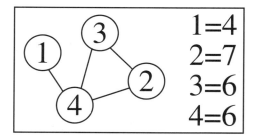

1=4
2=7
3=6
4=6

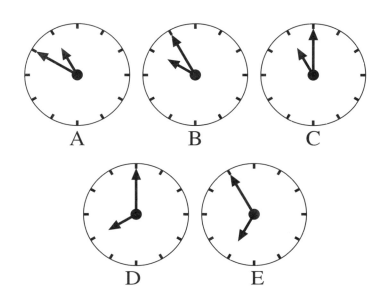

What comes next?

Which of these is not a DRINK?

(a) SILLABUB

(b) MADEIRA

(c) ANISETTE

(d) GRENADA

What number should replace the ?

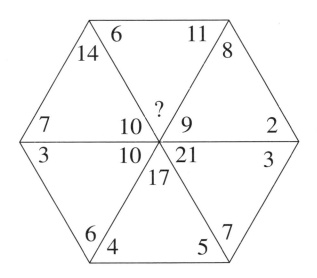

Each line and symbol which appears in the four outer circles, below, is transferred to the centre circle according to these rules. If a line or symbol occurs in the outer circles once, it is transferred; if it occurs twice, it is possibly transferred; three times, it is transferred; four times, it is not transferred. Which of the circles A, B, C, D or E, should appear at the centre of the diagram, below?

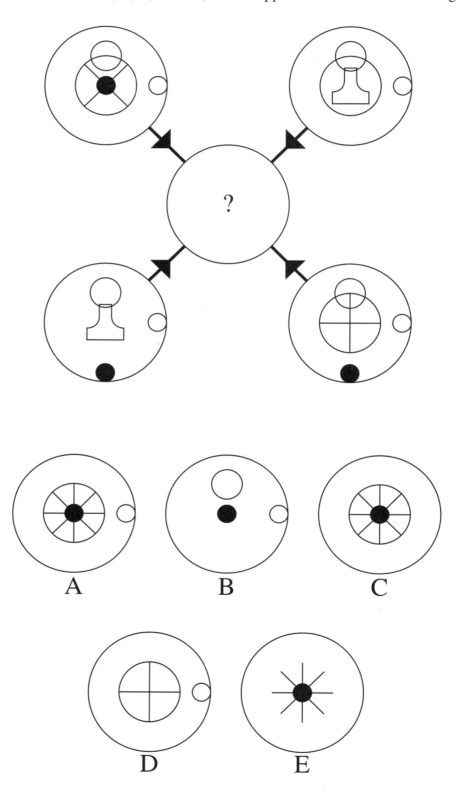

Which number will replace the ?

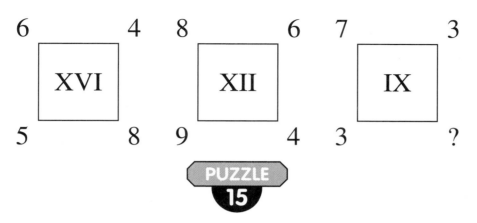

6   4   8   6   7   3

XVI   XII   IX

5   8   9   4   3   ?

Which is the odd one out?

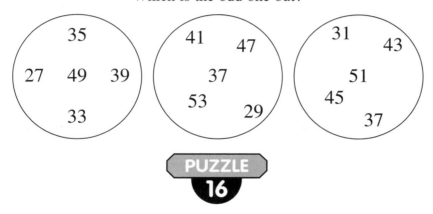

35
27   49   39
33

41   47
37
53   29

31   43
51
45
37

Which circle should replace the ?

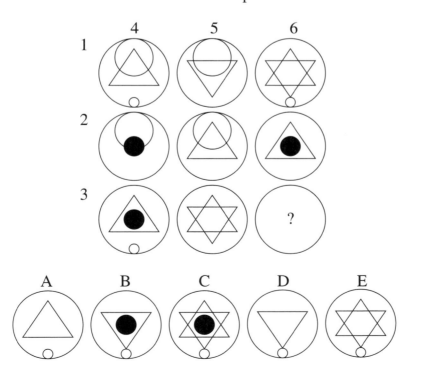

S E C T I O N

12

113

Which two words mean the same?

**INORDINATE,
CAPRICIOUS,
CONTINGENT,
REFORMATION,
OPULENCE,
FANCIFUL**

Which number is the odd one?

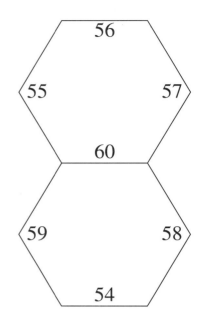

Which is the odd one out?

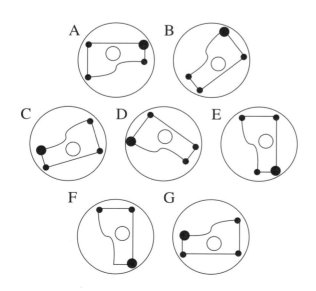

Which is the odd one out?

(a) ENDIVE

(b) FENNEL

(c) MACAQUE

(d) PIMENTO

(e) SEAKALE

PUZZLE 21

What is the name given to a group of MULES?

(a) BARREN
(b) COLONY
(c) CLUTTER
(d) FLUSH
(e) KNOB

PUZZLE 22

If 52 = 64

and

36 = x

What is the value of x?

PUZZLE 23

Which word is the odd word?

(a) HOWLER
(b) CROCODILE
(c) DESTITUTE
(d) DEMURE
(e) CARBON

PUZZLE 24

What is GRAUPEL?

(a) FLOWER
(b) GERMAN SAUSAGE
(c) FROZEN RAIN
(d) INSECT
(e) HINGED FLAP

Each line and symbol which appears in the four outer circles, below, is transferred to the centre circle according to these rules. If a line or symbol occurs in the outer circles once, it is transferred; if it occurs twice, it is possibly transferred; three times, it is transferred; four times, it is not transferred. Which of the circles A, B, C, D or E, should appear at the centre of the diagram, below?

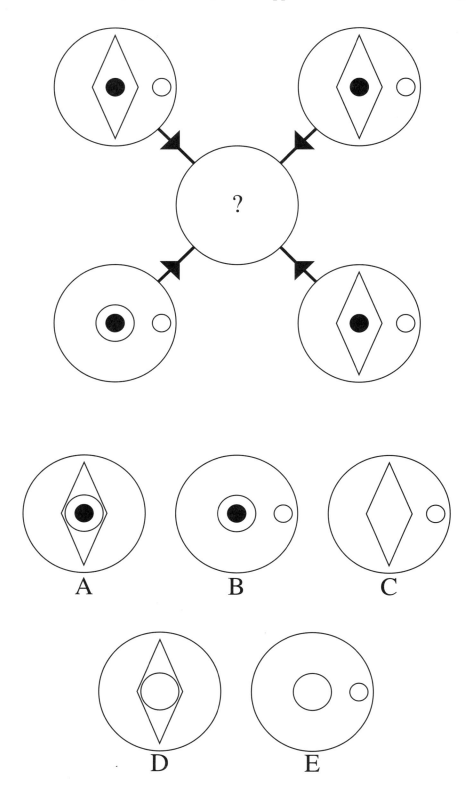

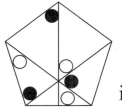

PUZZLE 1

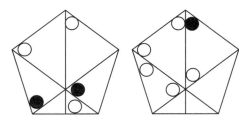

is to:

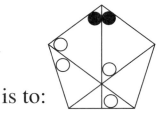

as:

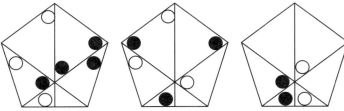

is to:

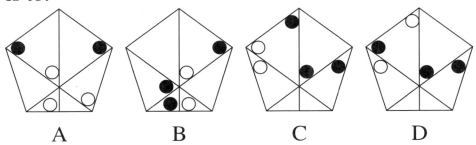

A   B   C   D

PUZZLE 2

Out of 100 people surveyed, 75 percent had a personal computer, 68 percent had a dishwasher, 85 percent had a refrigerator and 80 percent had a video recorder.

How many people had all four items?

PUZZLE 3

Which is the odd one out?

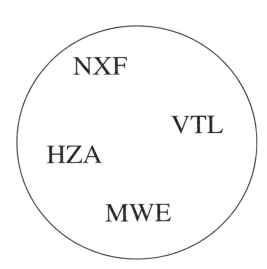

PUZZLE 4

What square should replace the question mark?

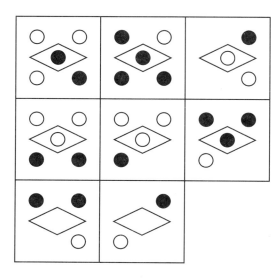

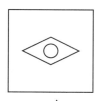 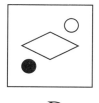 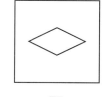

A   B   C

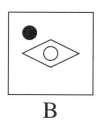 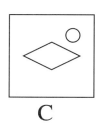 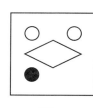

D   E   F

PUZZLE 5

Which is the odd one out?

54   24   17

36   14   51

18   72   12

PUZZLE 6

is to:

as:

is to:

  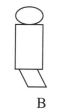

A   B   C

 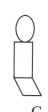

D   E

The seventh batsman to be out in the innings has scored 36 runs, which raises the average for all seven batsmen dismissed from 15 to 18. How many would the seventh batsman have needed to score to raise the team average to 20?

6384 is to **183**

and

3258 is to **108**

and

6191 is to **611**

therefore

3194 is to **?**

Insert the numbers into the grid, so that all calculations are correct both across and down. 6 and 8 already placed.

	x		=	6
+		+		÷
	-		=	
=		=		=
8	-		=	

How many lines appear below?

Each line and symbol which appears in the four outer circles, below, is transferred to the centre circle according to these rules. If a line or symbol occurs in the outer circles once, it is transferred; if it occurs twice, it is possibly transferred; three times, it is transferred; four times, it is not transferred. Which of the circles A, B, C, D or E, should appear at the centre of the diagram, below?

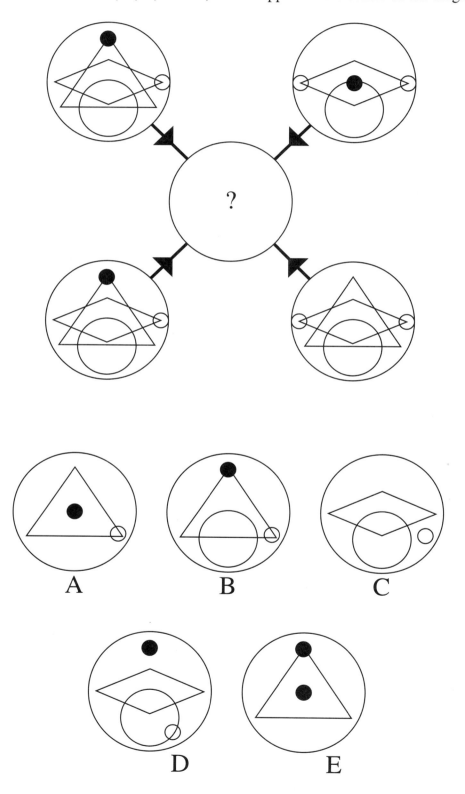

PUZZLE 12

Which circle should replace the ?

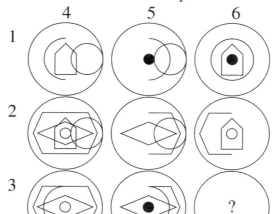

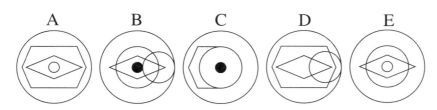

PUZZLE 13

What number should replace the ?

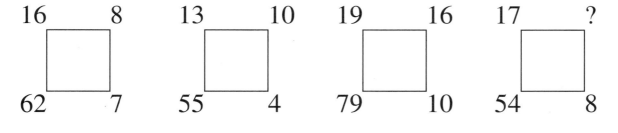

PUZZLE 14

What number should replace the ?

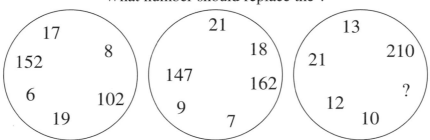

PUZZLE 15

Can you replace the ?'s with the signs x or ÷ to make it total 60?

18 ? 6 ? 2 ? 1 ? 10 = 60

PUZZLE 16

What is the name given to a group of TEAL?

(a) MUSTER
(b) MURDER
(c) KNOB
(d) KNOT
(e) GLEAN

PUZZLE 17

Which two words mean the same?

COGITATE,
PORTENT,
INDIGENCE,
INDICATION,
INTRACTIBLE,
SUPERIFICAL

PUZZLE 18

Which letter should replace the ?

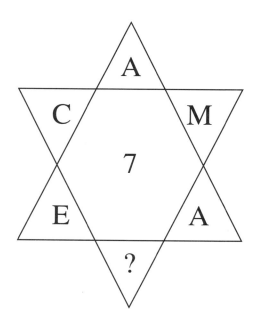

A

C   M

7

E   A

?

PUZZLE 19

Which word is the opposite of ZEPHYR?

(a) JARGON   (b) SQUALL   (c) TERMAGENT

(d) MANIFESTATION

PUZZLE 20

What number should replace the ?

6	4	7	2	1	1	2	7	4
6	6	4	7	2	1	1	2	7
4	6	6	4	7	2	?	1	4

PUZZLE 21

What are GALLIGASKINS?

(a) VEHICLES (b) WARMING PANS

(c) SMALL COLOURED FLAGS (d) TYPE OF HAY

(e) BREECHES

PUZZLE 22

Change 131 F to Celsius

PUZZLE
23

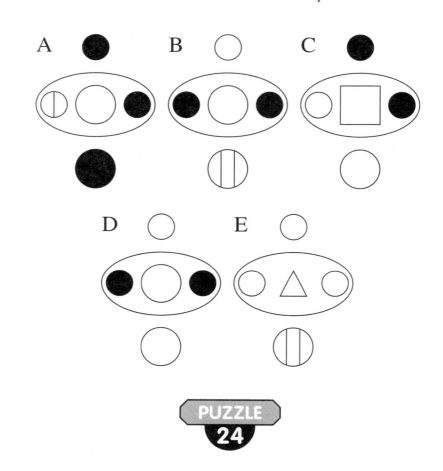

What comes next in the above sequence?

A

B

C

D

E

PUZZLE
24

Which word is the opposite of VALOROUS?

(a) UNSULLIED
(b) PUNCTILIOUS

(c) TIMID
(d) FAWN

Each line and symbol which appears in the four outer circles, below, is transferred to the centre circle according to these rules. If a line or symbol occurs in the outer circles once, it is transferred; if it occurs twice, it is possibly transferred; three times, it is transferred; four times, it is not transferred. Which of the circles A, B, C, D or E, should appear at the centre of the diagram, below?

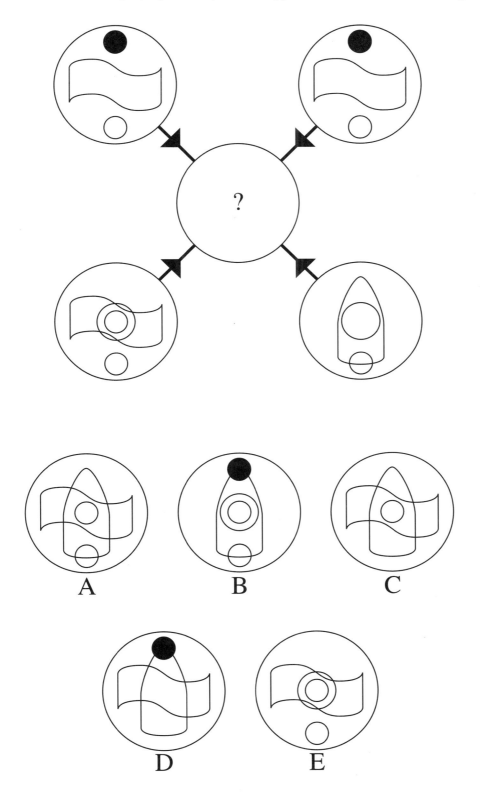

A   B   C

D   E

PUZZLE 1

Which is the odd one out?

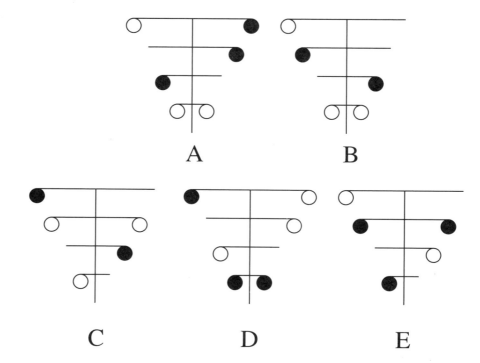

A B

C D E

PUZZLE 2

Find the value of x

| 18 |
| 31 |
| 21 1/4 |
| 26 3/4 |
| 24 1/2 |
| 22 1/2 |
| 27 3/4 |
| x |

PUZZLE 3

Which is the odd one out?

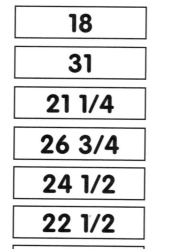

A

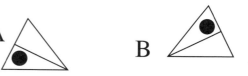
B

C

D

E

PUZZLE 4

A B C D E F G H

What letter is three to the left of the letter which comes midway between the letter two to the right of the letter A and the letter three to the right of the letter D?

PUZZLE 5

What number should replace the question mark?

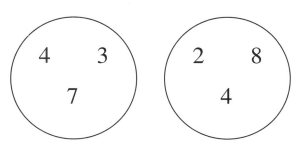

4   3
  7

2   8
   4

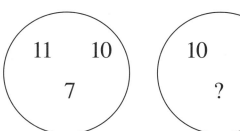

11   10
   7

10   6
   ?

PUZZLE 6

Which is the odd one out?

1	2	3	4	5
6	7	8	9	10
11	12	13	14	15

PUZZLE 7

What number should replace the question mark?

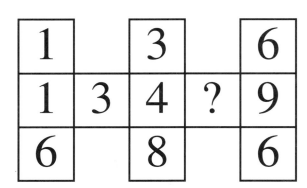

PUZZLE 8

What number should replace the question mark?

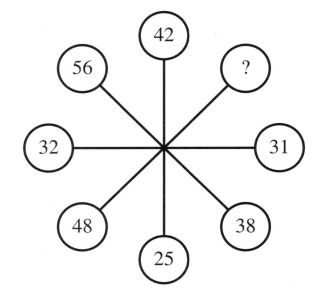

PUZZLE 9

In how many ways can the word TURN be read? Start at the central letter T and move in any direction.

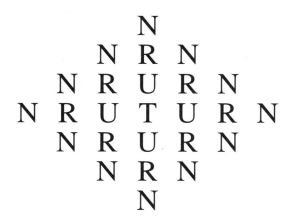

PUZZLE 10

Which is the odd one out?

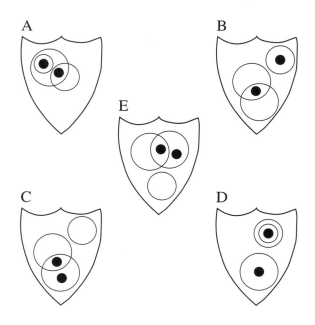

Each line and symbol which appears in the four outer circles, below, is transferred to the centre circle according to these rules. If a line or symbol occurs in the outer circles once, it is transferred; if it occurs twice, it is possibly transferred; three times, it is transferred; four times, it is not transferred. Which of the circles A, B, C, D or E, should appear at the centre of the diagram, below?

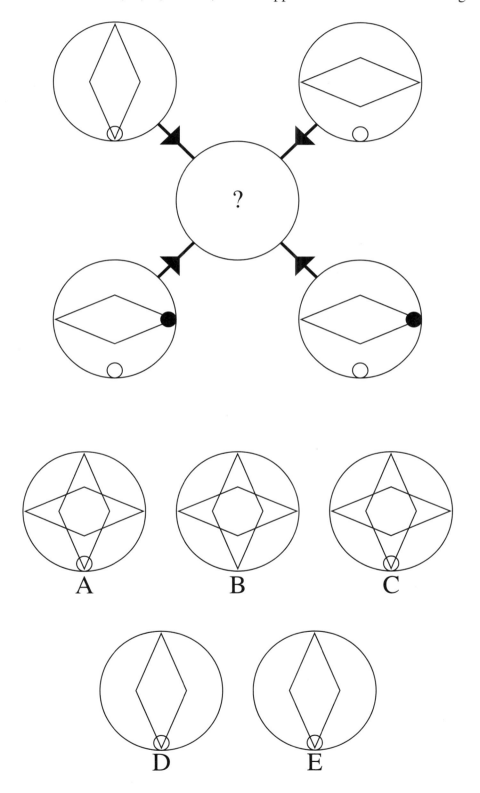

A   B   C

D   E

PUZZLE
12

Which Pentagons are the odd two out?

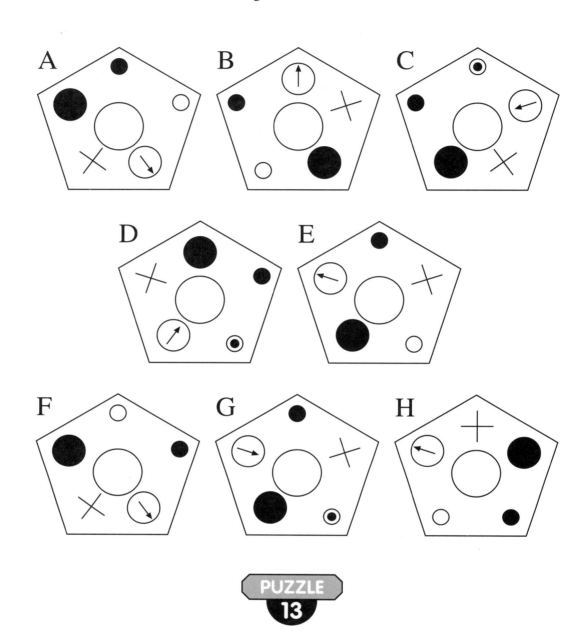

PUZZLE
13

What number should replace the ?

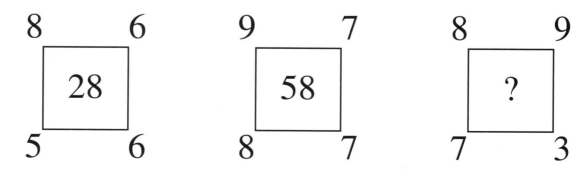

Which circle should replace the ?

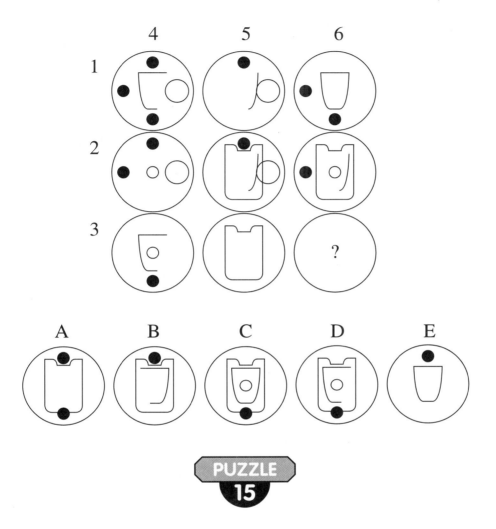

	4	5	6
1			
2			
3			?

A   B   C   D   E

Which is the odd one out?

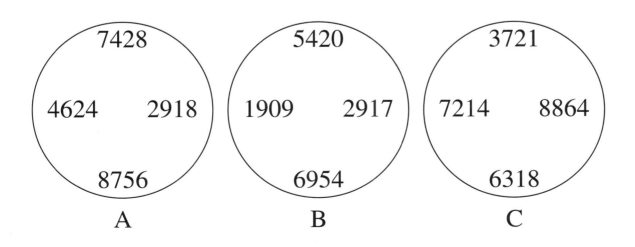

A	B	C
7428	5420	3721
4624 2918	1909 2917	7214 8864
8756	6954	6318

S
E
C
T
I
O
N

14

PUZZLE
16

What number should replace the ?

PUZZLE
17

What number should replace the ?

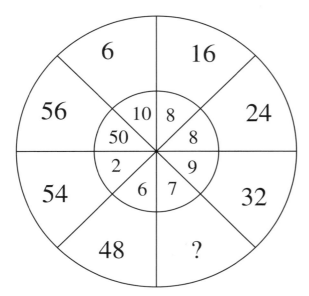

7	9	4	64
8	5	5	65
2	4	11	66
5	6	2	?

PUZZLE
18

What number should replace the ?

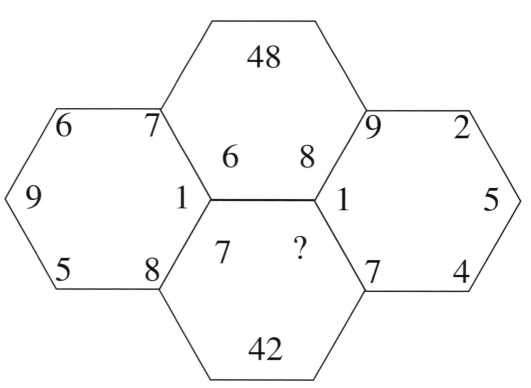

What is a GAUCHO?

(a) MINSTREL

(b) WINE

(c) BOAT

(d) FISH

(e) COWBOY

Which two words mean the opposite?

DELINEATION,
DISSIPATE,
ILLUSION,
DISCONCERT,
DERANGE,
SAVE

What number should replace the ?

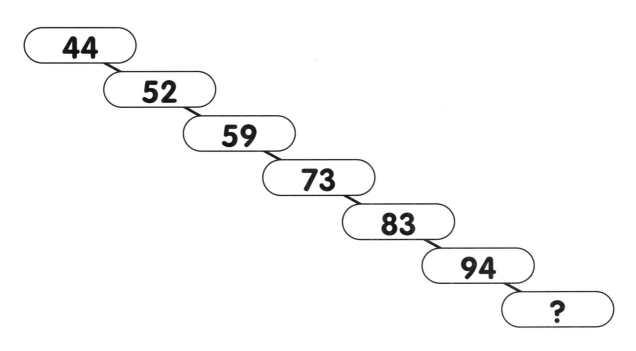

44

52

59

73

83

94

?

S E C T I O N

14

PUZZLE 22

Find the decimal for

$$\frac{276}{1656}$$

PUZZLE 23

What is always part of a TILBURY?

(a) CLOTH
(b) METAL
(c) TRACERY
(d) LIQUID
(e) WHEELS

PUZZLE 24

What is JACOBUS?

(a) GOLD COIN

(b) CLOTH

(c) PLANT

(d) FISH

(e) SWORD

PUZZLE 25

Which is the odd one out?
Clue: Colours

(a) NORMAO
(b) KINPHIS
(c) SETSUR
(d) DIRIIUM
(e) SHIBLU

PUZZLE 1

Which is the missing piece?

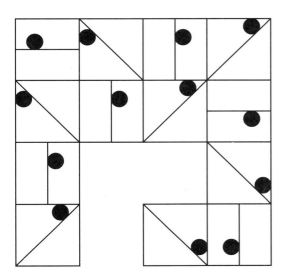

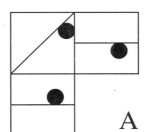 A

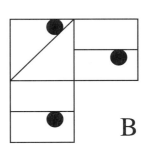 B

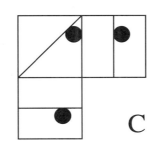 C

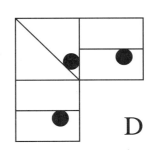 D

PUZZLE 2

At a recent election, a total of 96347 votes were cast for the four candidates, the winner exceeding his opponents by 10496, 21221 and 34628 votes respectively.

How many votes were cast for each candidate?

PUZZLE 3

A B C D E F G H

What letter is immediately to the right of the letter two to the right of the letter immediately to the left of the letter three to the right of the letter B?

S
E
C
T
I
O
N

15

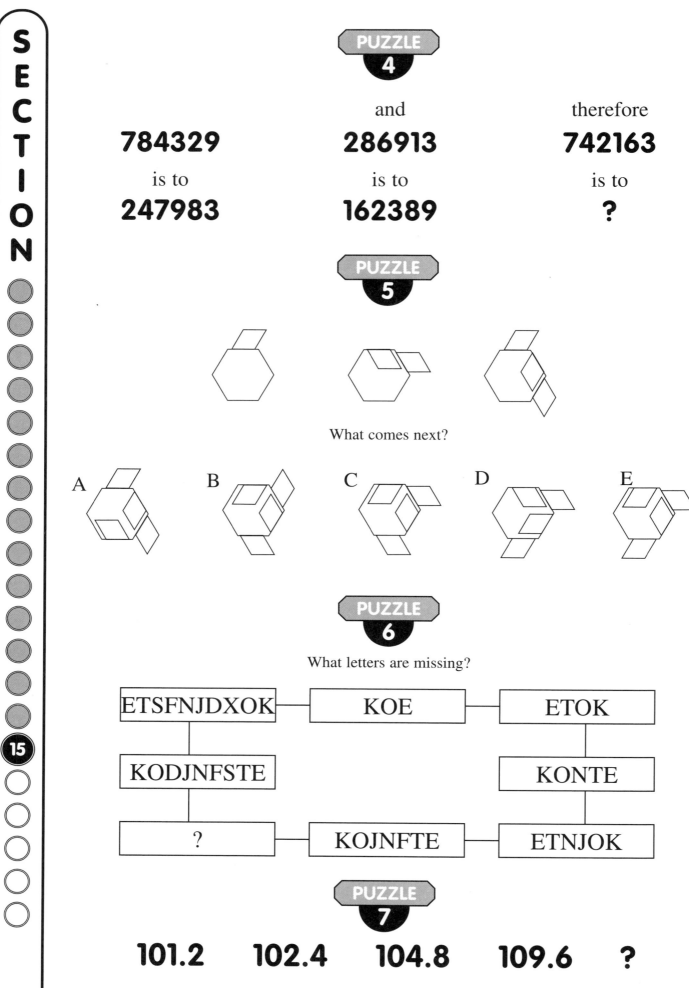

PUZZLE 4

784329

and

286913

therefore

742163

is to

247983

is to

162389

is to

?

PUZZLE 5

What comes next?

A   B   C   D   E

PUZZLE 6

What letters are missing?

ETSFNJDXOK	KOE	ETOK
KODJNFSTE		KONTE
?	KOJNFTE	ETNJOK

PUZZLE 7

101.2   102.4   104.8   109.6   ?

What numbers should replace the question marks?

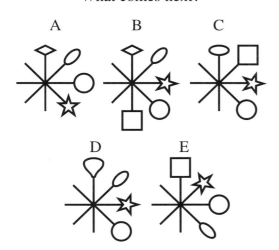

What comes next?

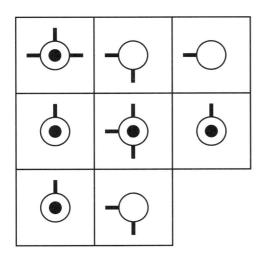

A	B	C	D
2	3	5	7
7	8	9	10
16	17	17	18
?	?	?	?

PUZZLE 10

Which is the missing tile?

A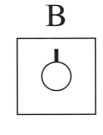

B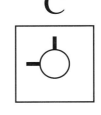

C

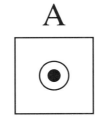

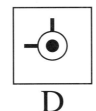
D

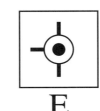
E

F

Each line and symbol which appears in the four outer circles, below, is transferred to the centre circle according to these rules. If a line or symbol occurs in the outer circles once, it is transferred; if it occurs twice, it is possibly transferred; three times, it is transferred; four times, it is not transferred. Which of the circles A, B, C, D or E, should appear at the centre of the diagram, below?

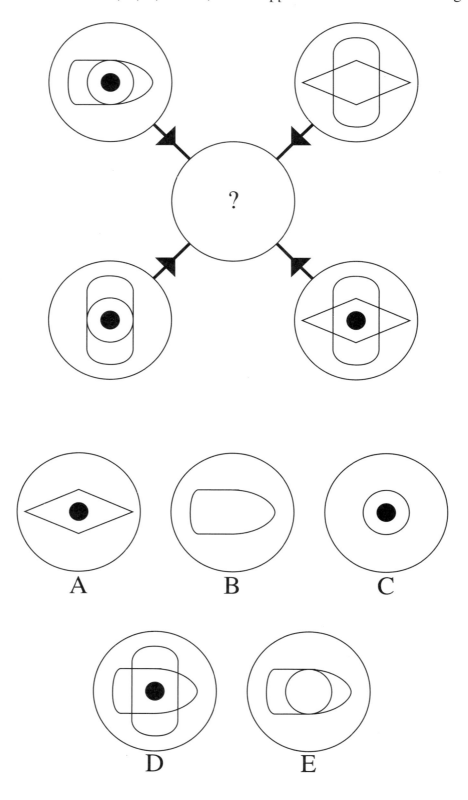

PUZZLE
12

Which 2 pentagons are the odd ones out?

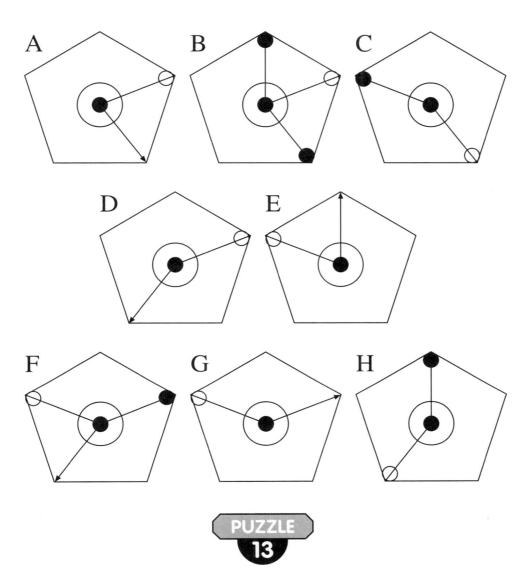

PUZZLE
13

Which number replaces the ?

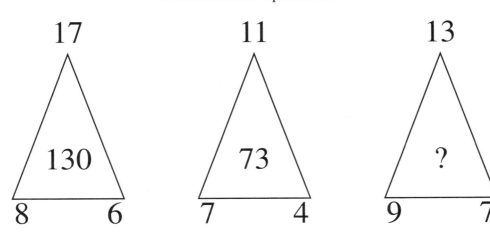

PUZZLE 14

Which hexagon replaces the ? A, B, C, D or E?

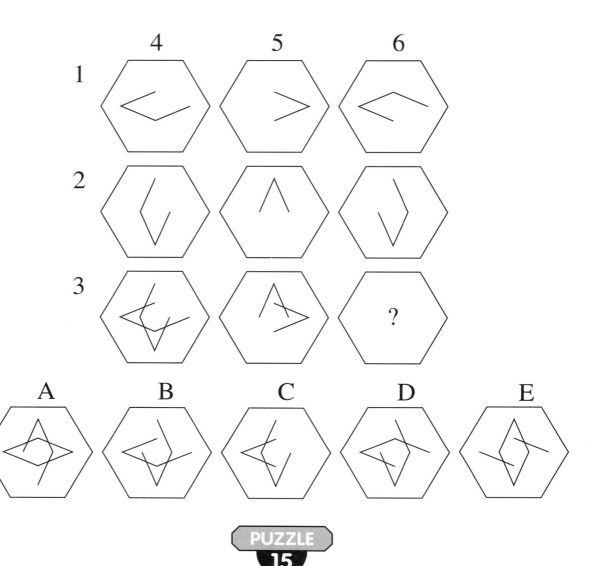

PUZZLE 15

What number should replace the ?

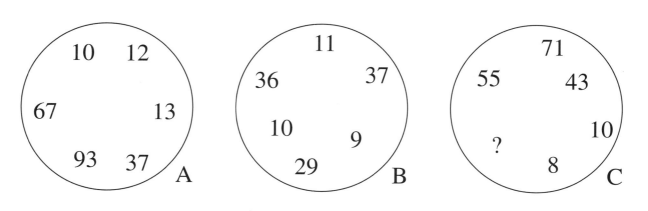

PUZZLE 16

What is the value of this angle?

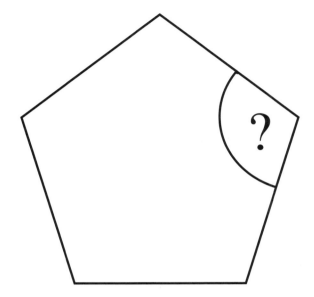

PUZZLE 17

Simplify

$$\frac{3024}{3888}$$

PUZZLE 18

What have these words in common?

**DIMENSIONS
GRANDIOSE
REMARKABLE
DESCENT
MATERIAL
RESOUNDED**

PUZZLE 19

12 matches are arranged to produce 6 triangles. Move 5 matches to produce 3 triangles?

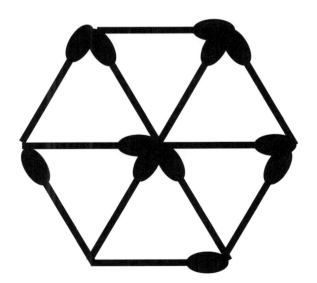

PUZZLE
20

Which playing card replaces the ?

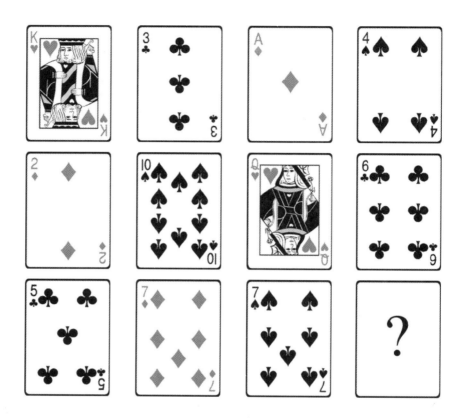

PUZZLE
21

Which watch completes the sequence?

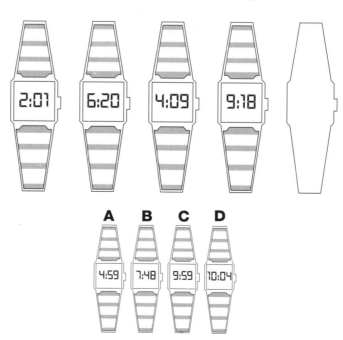

A   B   C   D

What number should replace the ?

7	9	6	57
8	6	7	41
9	3	4	23
10	6	11	?

What is a CAPELIN?

(a) A RELIGIOUS PERSON
(b) A WEAPON
(c) A FISH
(d) A BIRD
(e) A CAPE

Which is higher?

19^2

or

7^3

Simplify

$$\frac{99}{16} \div \frac{11}{4} =$$

S
E
C
T
I
O
N

143

PUZZLE 1

Which is the odd one out?

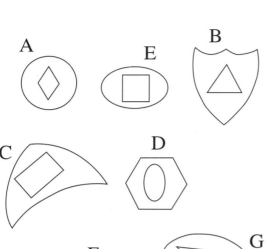

A   E   B

C   D

F   G

PUZZLE 2

Which is the odd one out?
4789
3568
1458
2479
2548
4679
2378

PUZZLE 3

Which is the meteorological sign for hail?

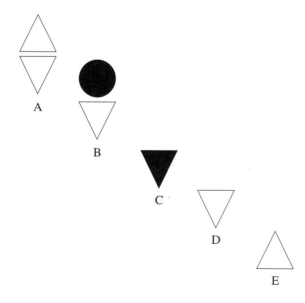

A   B   C   D   E

PUZZLE 4

Insert the missing numbers. The connection between each set of numbers in each row is the same.

623	36	?

847	?	16

726	?	?

PUZZLE 5

What letter should replace the question mark?

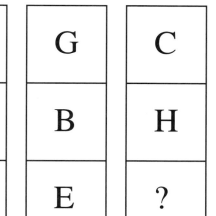

A	G	C
B	B	H
C	E	?

PUZZLE 6

121
2112
2122
1132
211213
312213
212223
?

PUZZLE 7

What comes next?

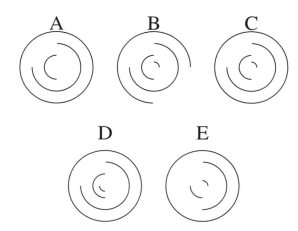

A   B   C

D   E

PUZZLE 8

The shapes contain five consecutive numbers (in no particular order) as indicated by the question marks.

When added together:
The numbers in the triangle = 53
The numbers in the circle = 79
The numbers in the square = 50
The total of the five numbers = 130

What numbers should replace the question marks?

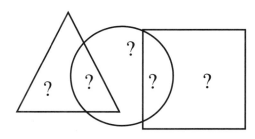

S
E
C
T
I
O
N

16

145

PUZZLE 9

What number should replace the question mark?

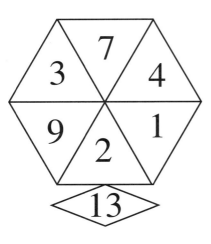

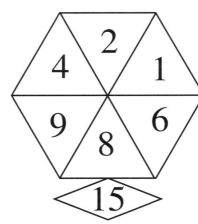

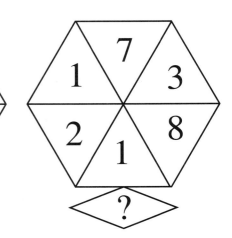

PUZZLE 10

Which is the missing piece?

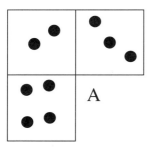

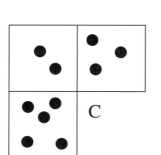

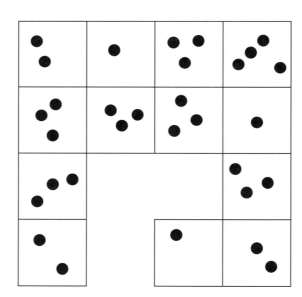

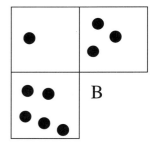

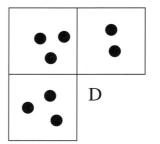

Each line and symbol which appears in the four outer circles, below, is transferred to the centre circle according to these rules: If a line or symbol occurs in the outer circles: once: it is transferred twice: it is possibly transferred 3 times: it is transferred 4 times: it is not transferred. Which of the circles A, B, C, D or E, should appear at the centre of the diagram, below?

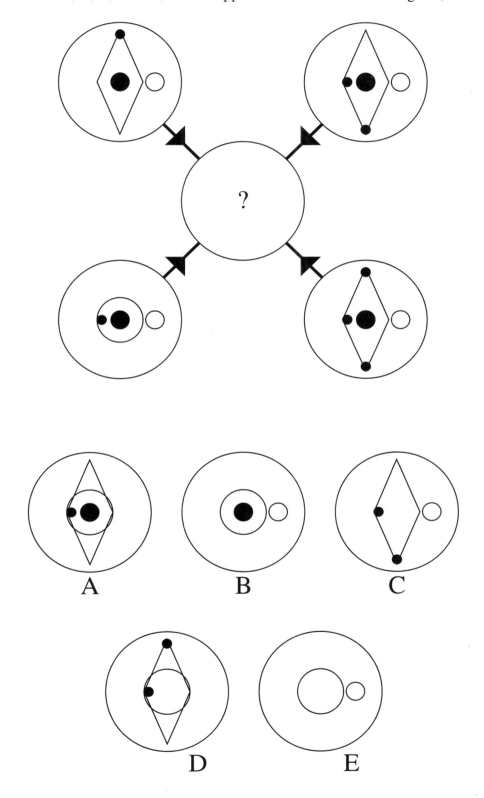

PUZZLE 12

Which playing card replaces the ?

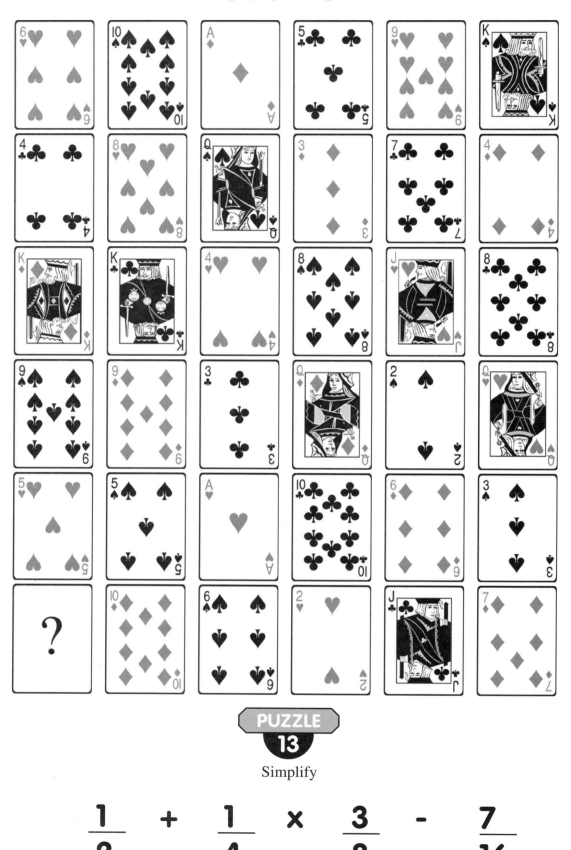

PUZZLE 13

Simplify

$$\frac{1}{2} + \frac{1}{4} \times \frac{3}{8} - \frac{7}{16}$$

PUZZLE 14

Which pentagons are the odd two out?

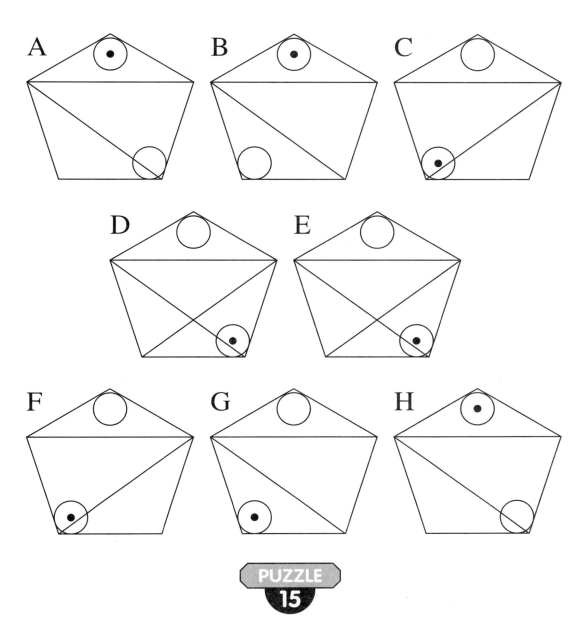

PUZZLE 15

What number should replace the ?

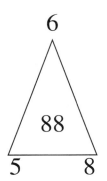 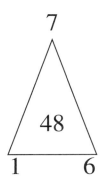 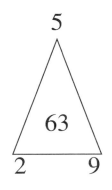 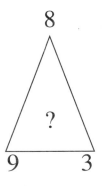

Find which hexagon fills the space to a definite rule.

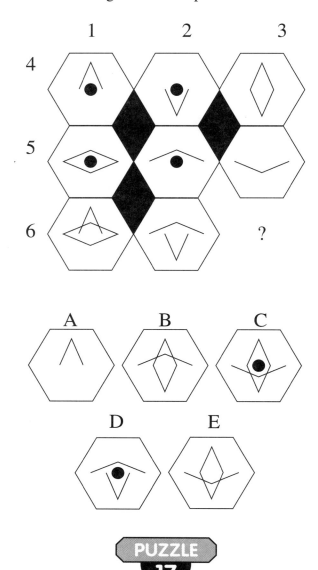

PUZZLE
17

Which is the odd one out, A, B or C?

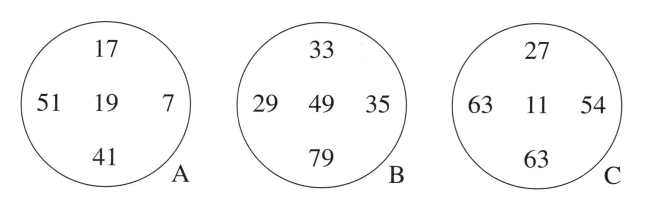

16

PUZZLE 18

Which letter of the alphabet should replace the ?

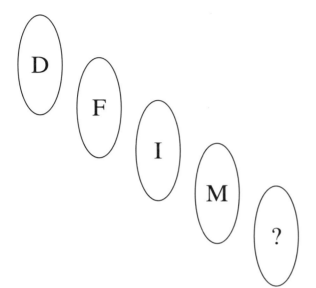

D

F

I

M

?

PUZZLE 19

What is the meaning of MILIEU?

(a) DISCORD
(b DISORDER
(c) MARRIAGE
(d) HAPPINESS
(e) ENVIRONMENT

PUZZLE 20

Which word means the opposite of PULCHRITUDE?

(a) UGLINESS
(b) BEAUTY
(c) REALITY
(d) SWEETNESS
(e) ARCHAIC

PUZZLE 21

What number should replace the ?

1   80   9

3   40   7

5   ?   6

PUZZLE 22

What number will replace the ?

A	B	C	D
17	18	16	31
23	60	25	37
39	44	36	?
47	28	49	43
81	32	64	47

PUZZLE 23

What is CANASTER?

(a) A TOBACCO
(b) A CARD GAME
(c) A DANCE
(d) A VASE
(e) A BOLD LINE

PUZZLE 24

Which of the following is always part of BANNOCK?

(a) OATMEAL
(b) CELERY
(c) MUSTARD
(d) CHOCOLATE
(e) CARROTS

PUZZLE 25

What numbers should replace the ?'s

78	930	15
29	400	11
37	?	?

PUZZLE 1

When the pattern below is folded to form a cube
which is the only one of the following that can be produced?

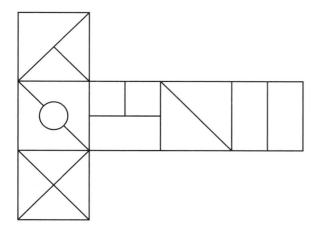

A   B   C

 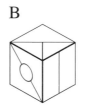 

D   E

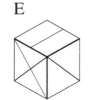

PUZZLE 2

Insert the missing numbers. The connection between each set of numbers in each row is the same.

196	114	?
376	?	44
487	?	?

PUZZLE 3

What should be the missing numbers?

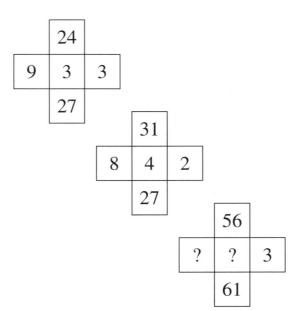

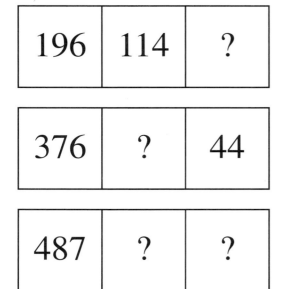

PUZZLE 4

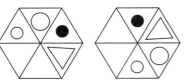

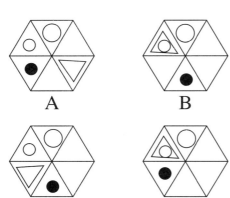

What comes next?

PUZZLE 5

What should be the missing number?

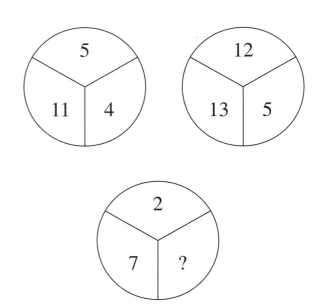

PUZZLE 6

What should be the missing letter?

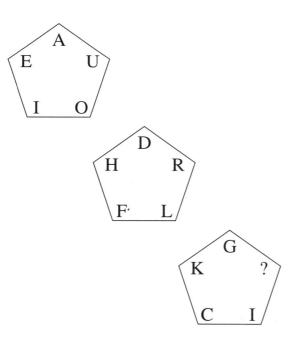

PUZZLE 7

Which is the odd one out?

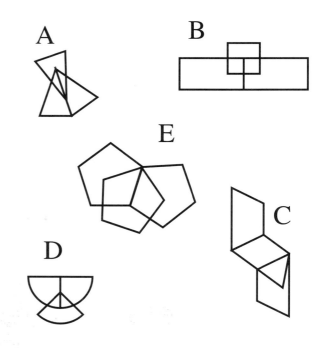

PUZZLE 8

What comes next?

15634

63451

45136

?

PUZZLE 9

What should be the missing number?

7
4 5 3
6

2
3 4 9
2

6
2 ? 8
8

PUZZLE 10

Which is the missing piece?

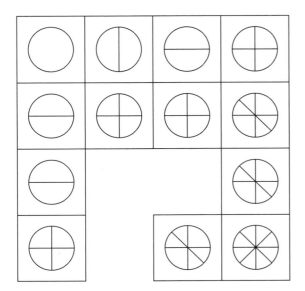

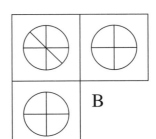
A

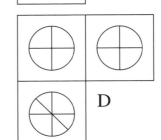
B

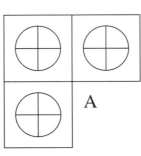
C

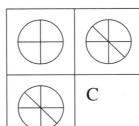
D

Each line and symbol which appears in the four outer circles, below, is transferred to the centre circle according to these rules: If a line or symbol occurs in the outer circles: once: it is transferred twice: it is possibly transferred   3 times: it is transferred   4 times: it is not transferred. Which of the circles A, B, C, D or E, should appear at the centre of the diagram, below?

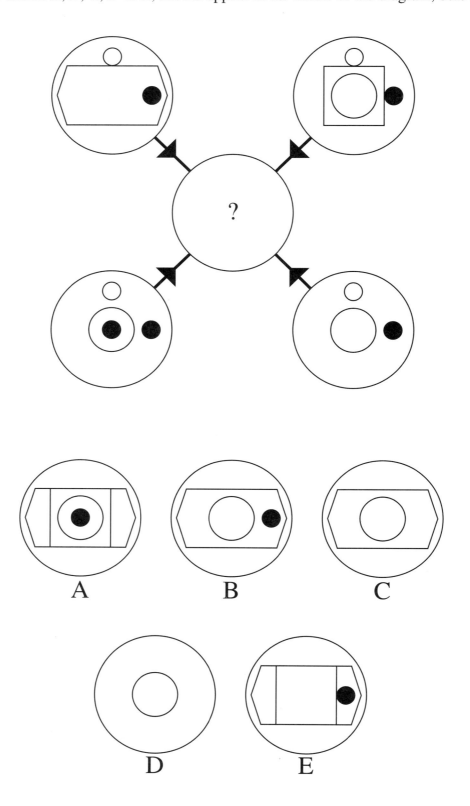

12

What number should replace the ?

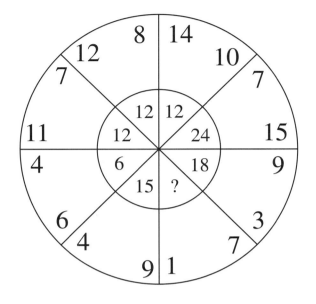

13

What is the meaning of CAJOLE?

(a) KNOCK
(b) WISH
(c) HESITATE
(d) LEAN
(e) COAX

14

If (15) (4²) = × (2³)

What does x = ?

(a) 28
(b) 30
(c) 32
(d) 34
(e) 36

15

What is the drawing for no.6?

9   1   5   4

7   2   8   3

PUZZLE
16

Which hexagonal replaces the ?
A, B, C, D or E?

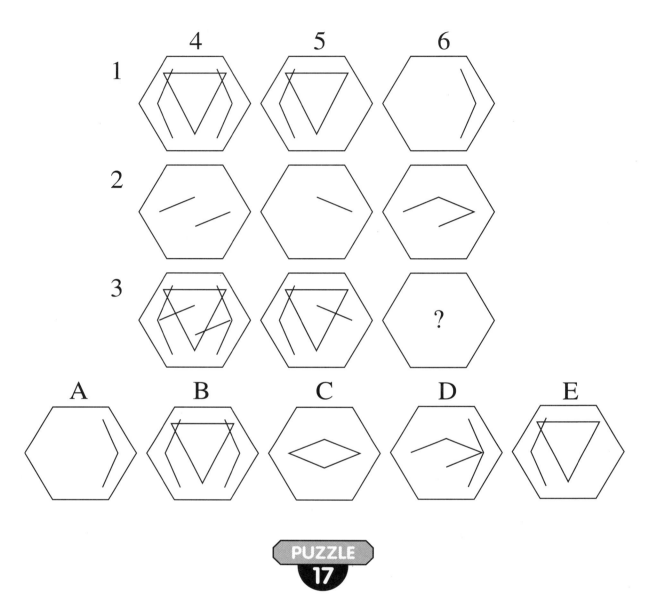

PUZZLE
17

What number should replace the ?

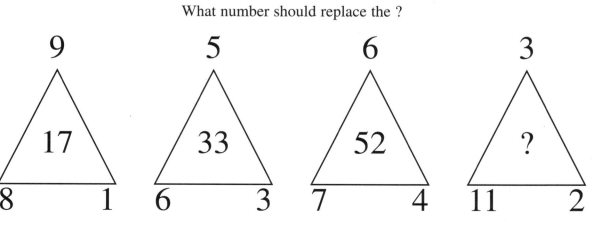

Find the circle to replace the ?

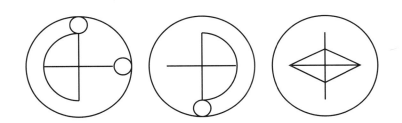

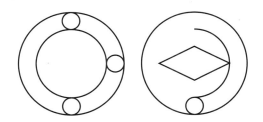

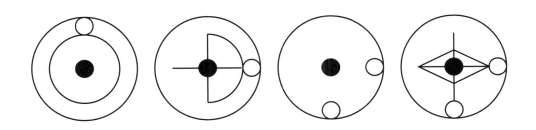

A	B	C	D	E

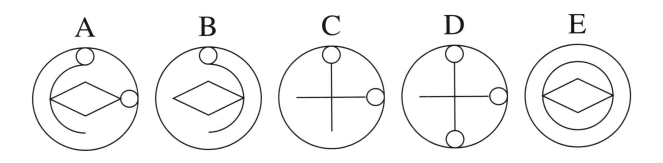

S E C T I O N

17

160

PUZZLE 19

What number should replace the ?

37
9   4 1
2

11
26   19
33

46
2   4 1
?

PUZZLE 20

If coke costs 74p and milk costs 63p and beer costs 78p

What does lime cost?

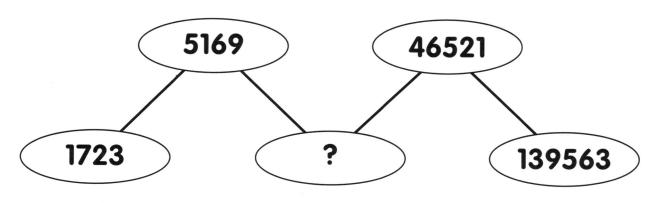

PUZZLE 21

Which number replaces the ? in this sequence?

5169   46521

1723   ?   139563

What number should replace the ?

5	4	6	2	4	1	7	8	7
6	6	4	2	2	7	8	?	1
5	2	7	1	2	7	6	5	4

What is the square root (√) of 3249?

(a) 47   (b) 53   (c) 57   (d) 63   (e) 67

Which of these is not a SEA?

Which number should replace the ?

126   3   24

364   4   19

(a) BERING

(b) WEDDELL

(c) ANAPURNA

98   ?   41

(d) TIMOR

Which is the odd one out?

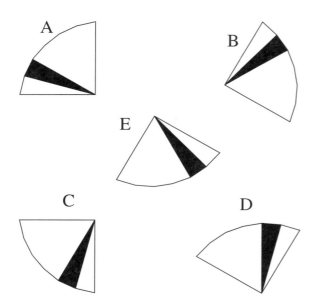

What number should replace the question mark?

1	2	2
1	1	4
2	3	?

Which set of letters is the odd one out?

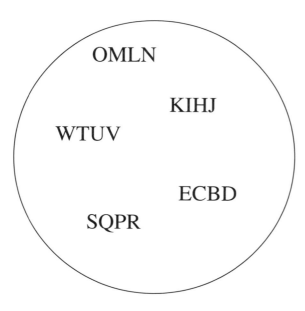

OMLN

KIHJ

WTUV

ECBD

SQPR

The three cog wheels are in contact with each other. The number of cogs on each is shown on each wheel. How many revolutions must be made by the largest wheel before all of the cogs are returned to their original start positions?

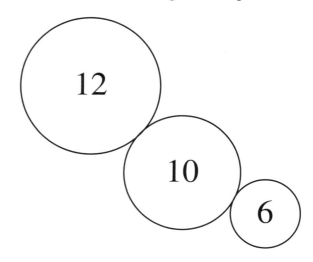

12

10

6

PUZZLE 5

When the pattern below is folded to form a cube,
which is the only one of the following that can be produced?

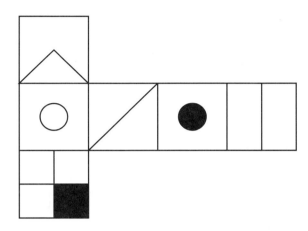

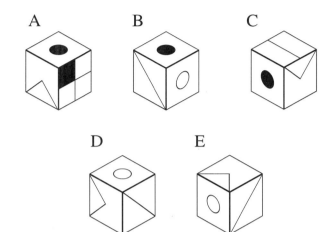

A   B   C

D   E

PUZZLE 6

What number should replace the question mark?

723 — 168 — 489

637 — 67 — 429

453 — ? — 245

PUZZLE 7

What number comes next?

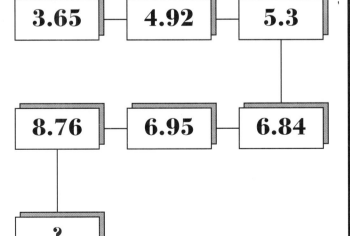

3.65 — 4.92 — 5.3

8.76 — 6.95 — 6.84

?

PUZZLE
8

Which is the missing tile?

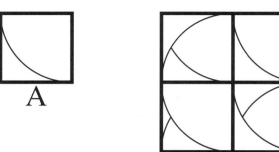

A

B

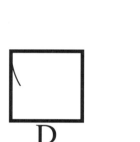

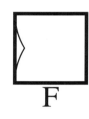

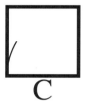

C

F

D

E

PUZZLE
9

Which is the missing piece?

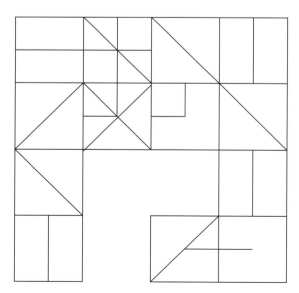

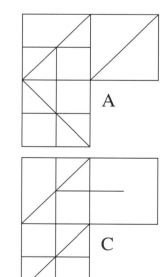

A

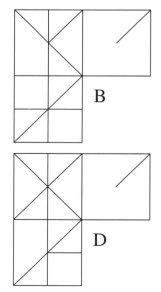

B

C

D

What number comes next?

58, 59.5, 89.25, 87.75, 89.25, 133.875, ?

Which letter should replace the ?

C	L	D
F	?	B
E	Y	E

PUZZLE 12

Each of the nine squares in the grid marked A1 to C3, should incorporate all the lines and symbols which are shown in the squares of the same letter and number immediately above and to the left. For example, B2 should incorporate all the lines and symbols that are in 2 and B. One of the squares is incorrect. Which one is it?

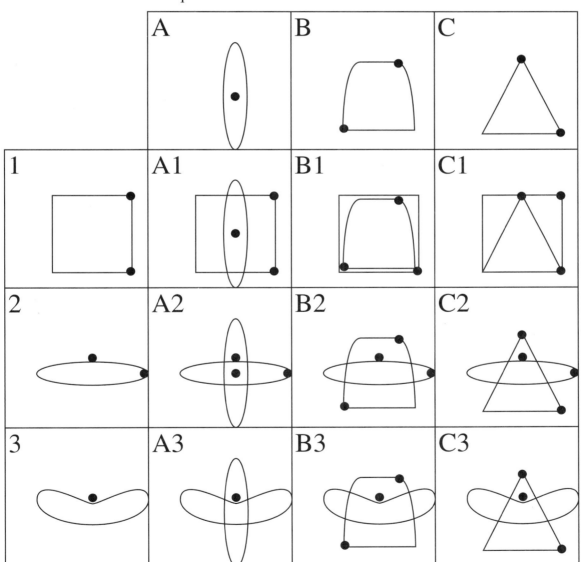

Each line and symbol which appears in the four outer circles, below, is transferred to the centre circle according to these rules: If a line or symbol occurs in the outer circles: once: it is transferred twice: it is possibly transferred 3 times: it is transferred 4 times: it is not transferred. Which of the circles A, B, C, D or E, should appear at the centre of the diagram, below?

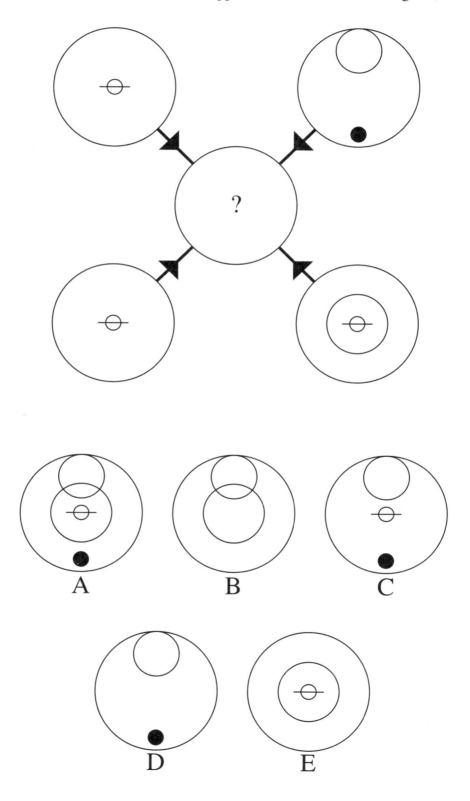

Which pentagon should replace the ?
A, B, C, D or E?

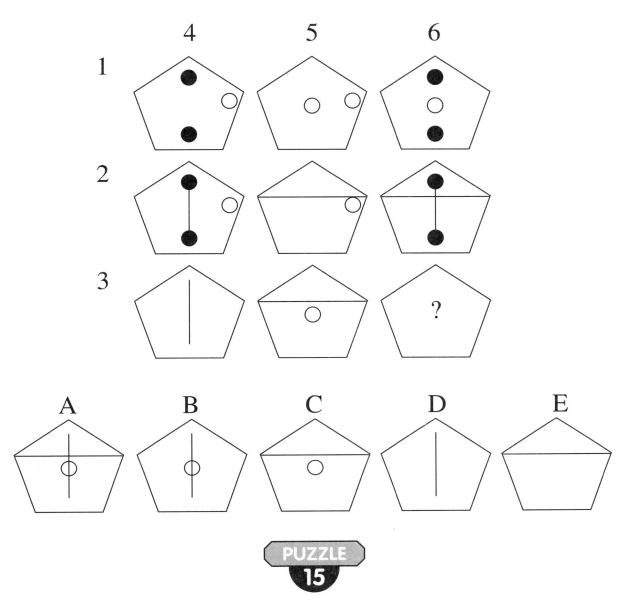

      4   5   6

A   B   C   D   E

Which number should replace the ?

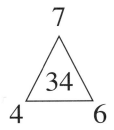
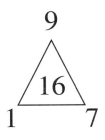
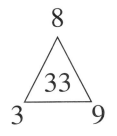
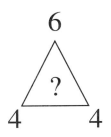

7   9   8   6

34   16   33   ?

4 6   1 7   3 9   4 4

SECTION

18

167

PUZZLE 16

What number should replace the ?

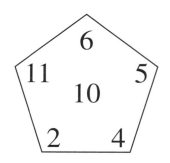

6
11   5
10
2   4

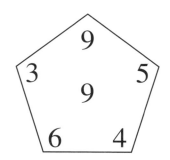

9
3   5
9
6   4

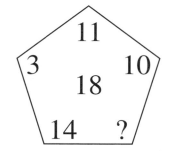

11
3   10
18
14   ?

PUZZLE 17

Which two words mean the opposite?

INDOLENT — **ERUDITION**

IMPOTENCE — **ILLITERACY**

EPICUREAN — **AUDACIOUS**

PUZZLE 18

Which playing card replaces the ?

What number replaces the ?

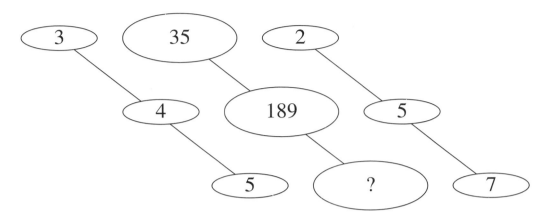

Solve the rebus (one word).

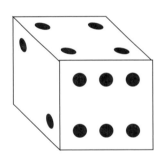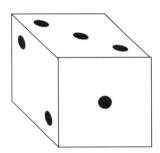

What number should replace the question mark?

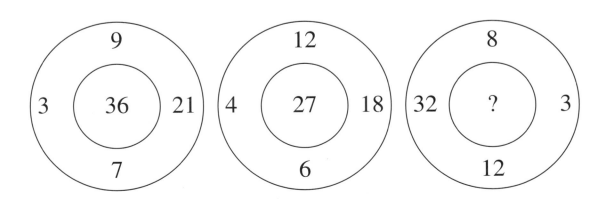

PUZZLE 22

Which is the odd one out?

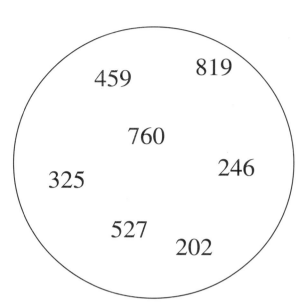

459   819

760

325   246

527

202

PUZZLE 23

What number comes next?

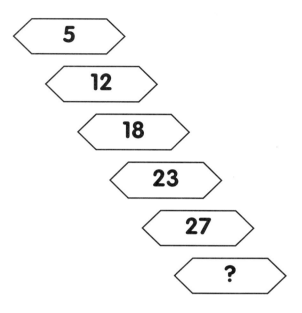

5

12

18

23

27

?

PUZZLE 24

Complete this table?

I	31	E
O	17	Y
?	23	O

PUZZLE 25

Which letter replaces the ?

C	D
J	F

E	H
Z	N

D	F
?	J

In a box of eggs 6 out of 52 are bad. What are the chances of drawing out 3 and finding them bad?

In a single week, each cat in the rat infested village of Catattackya killed the same number of rats as every other cat. The total number of rat fatalaties during the week came to 299.

Less than 20 cats achieved this remarkable feat. How many cats were there in Catattackya, and how many rats did each kill?

What number comes next?

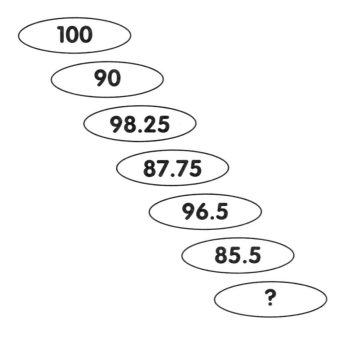

100

90

98.25

87.75

96.5

85.5

?

What comes next in this sequence?

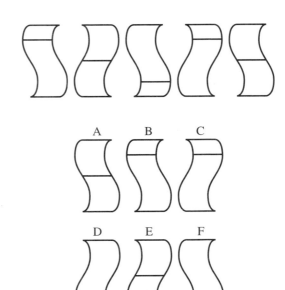

PUZZLE 5

What number comes next?

| 38 |
| 49 |
| 62 |
| 70 |
| ? |

PUZZLE 6

In the arrangement below, what is the difference between the sum of the three highest even numbers and the product of the two lowest odd numbers?

14	15	10	3
9	16	21	22
11	8	24	12

PUZZLE 7

Which is the odd one out?

A

B

C

D

E

What letter should replace the question mark?

N	L	O
I	M	K
Q	?	P

The combined ages of Frasier and Niles is 88 years

The combined ages of Niles and Daphne is 76 years

The combined ages of Frasier and Daphne is 80 years

Figure out each person's age.

What is the missing piece?

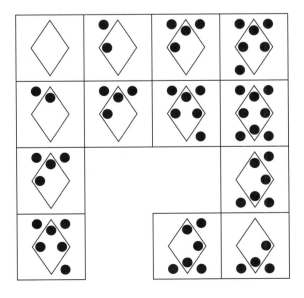

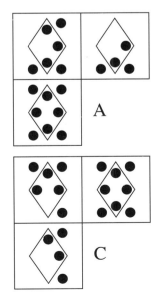

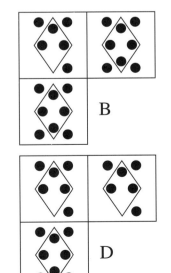

Each line and symbol which appears in the four outer circles, below, is transferred to the centre circle according to these rules: If a line or symbol occurs in the outer circles: once: it is transferred twice: it is possibly transferred   3 times: it is transferred 4 times: it is not transferred. Which of the circles A, B, C, D or E, should appear at the centre of the diagram, below?

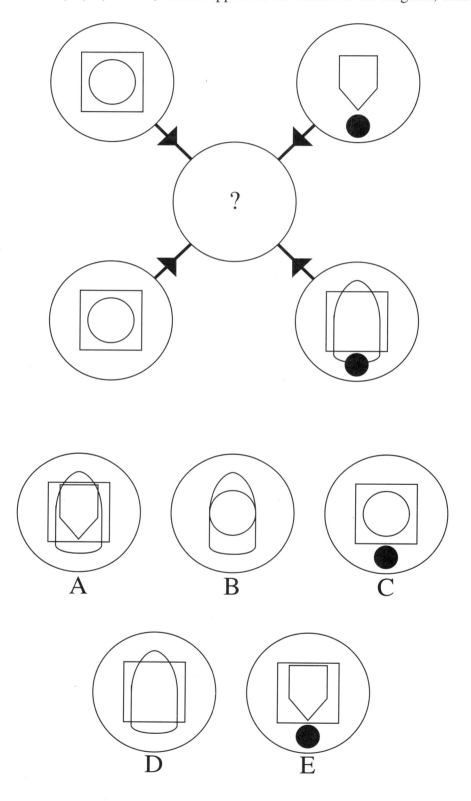

PUZZLE 12

What number should replace the ?

21	22	26	29
39	36	32	31
41	42	?	49
59	56	52	51

PUZZLE 13

In a sequence

6

-

18

-

54

find the 10th term.

PUZZLE 14

If

60 = 48

then

27 = ?

PUZZLE 15

What number should replace the ?

6 — (200) — 4

7 — (318) — 5

8 — (?) — 6

S E C T I O N

19

Each of the nine squares in the grid marked A1 to C3, should incorporate all the lines and symbols which are shown in the squares of the same letter and number immediately above and to the left. For example, B2 should incorporate all the lines and symbols that are in 2 and B. One of the squares is incorrect. Which one is it?

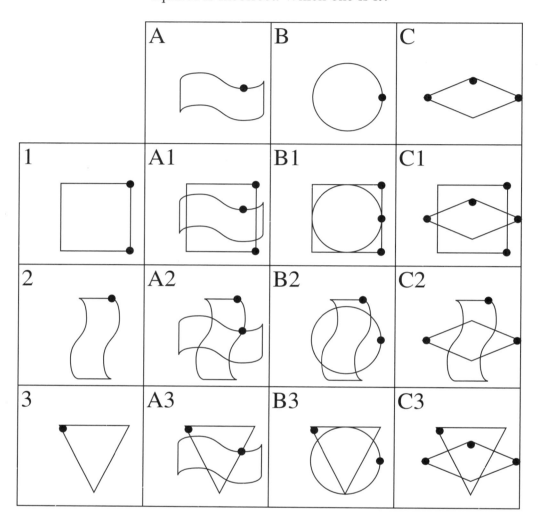

What number will replace the ?

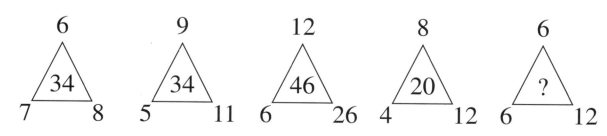

PUZZLE 18

What number should replace the ?

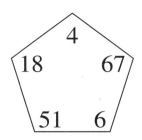

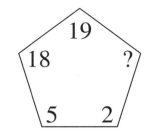

PUZZLE 19

Which pentagon A, B, C or D replaces the ?

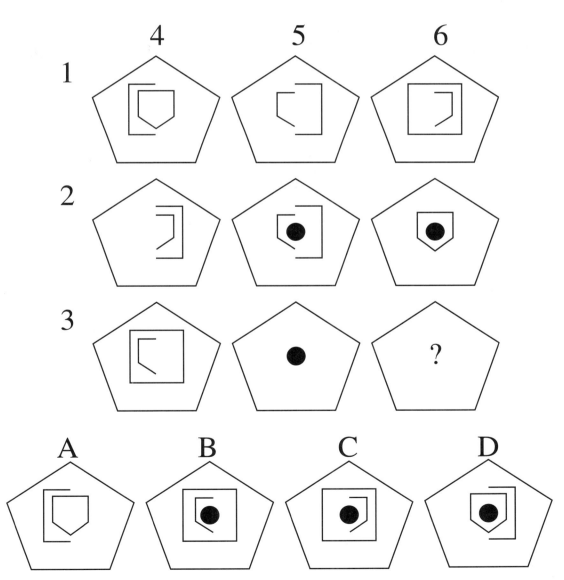

20

Which triangle should replace the ?

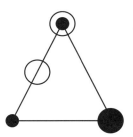 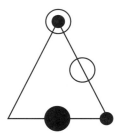 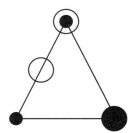 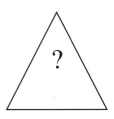

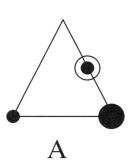
A

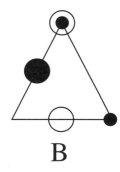
B

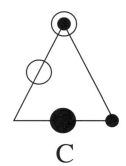
C

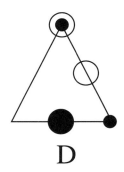
D

PUZZLE
21

Which letter is the odd one out?

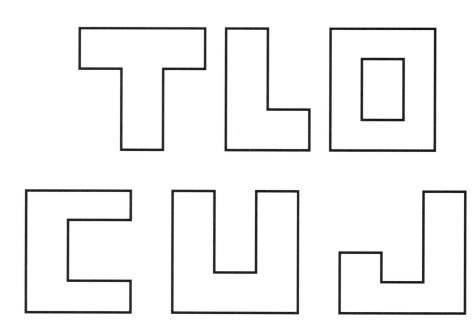

PUZZLE 22

Which number replaces the ?

5	4	12
6	2	5
3	8	?

PUZZLE 23

Which letter replaces the ?

D	R	F	
K	H	V	J
B	O	L	?
	F	S	P

PUZZLE 24

Which letter replaces the ?

H L
C Q
? U

PUZZLE 25

Which number is the odd one out?

741 64
423 194
132
549 411
14

SECTION

What is the missing tile?

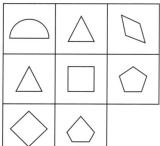

What is the missing letter?

A	D	C
J	I	F
G	?	E

A   B   C

D   E   F

PUZZLE 3

Which is the odd one out?

A

B

C

D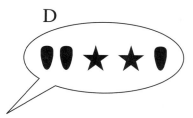

F

E

20

180

PUZZLE 4

What numbers should replace the question marks?

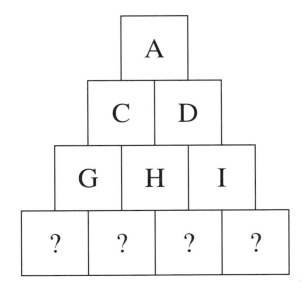

```
              A
          C       D
      G       H       I
  ?       ?       ?       ?
```

PUZZLE 5

What letter should replace the question mark?

A	B	C	D
B	D	F	H
C	F	I	L
D	H	L	?

PUZZLE 6

Which is the missing piece?

PUZZLE 7

In the arrangement below, what is the difference between the sum of the two highest odd numbers and the product of the two lowest even numbers?

19	4	18	17
16	22	27	10
21	8	15	6

PUZZLE 8

What should be the missing number?

2

5

5.75

7.75

9.5

10.5

?

PUZZLE 9

is to:

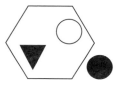

as:

is to:

A	B	C	D

  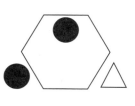 

What letter should replace the question mark?

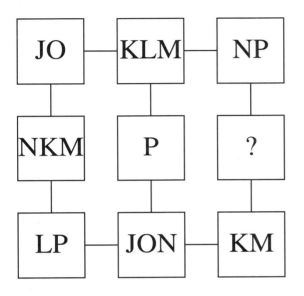

What number should replace the ?

?	3	6	1	4	6
6	1	1	1	2	3
1	2	5	0	2	3

Which hexagon should replace the ?

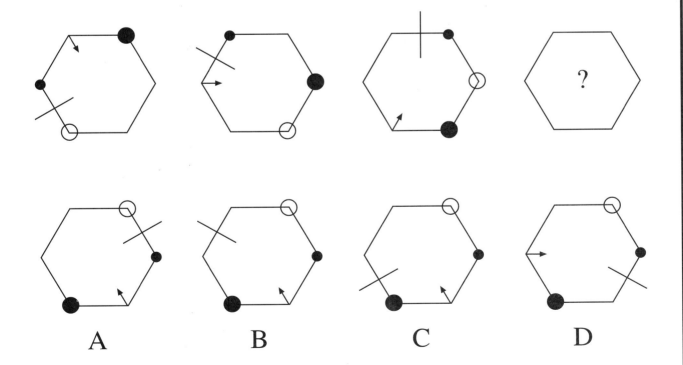

A   B   C   D

PUZZLE 13

What number should replace the ?

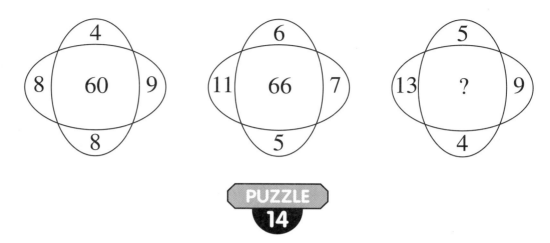

PUZZLE 14

Each of the nine squares in the grid marked A1 to C3, should incorporate all the lines and symbols which are shown in the squares of the same letter and number immediately above and to the left. For example, B2 should incorporate all the lines and symbols that are in 2 and B. One of the squares is incorrect. Which one is it?

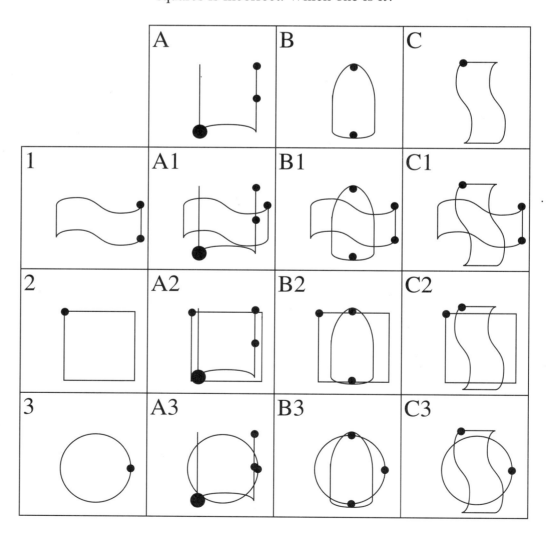

Which diagram has the most in common with A? B, C, D or E.

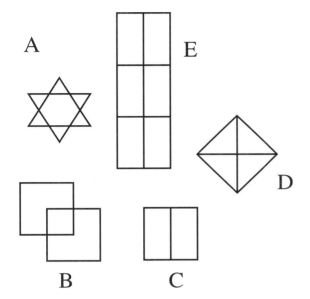

A
E
D
B   C

What is always part of a PUCK?

(a) CLOWN'S BOOTS
(b) RUBBER
(c) WOOD
(d) CHAIN MAIN

What have these words in common?

HALF-PENNY
RELIEVED
SHALLOT
PLENTIFUL
OPENED
PATRIOTIC

What number should replace the ?

16	14	5	67
7	109	93	21
11	32	?	61
41	7	21	4

SECTION

20

Each line and symbol which appears in the four outer circles, below, is transferred to the centre circle according to these rules: If a line or symbol occurs in the outer circles: once: it is transferred twice: it is possibly transferred 3 times: it is transferred 4 times: it is not transferred. Which of the circles A, B, C, D or E, should appear at the centre of the diagram, below?

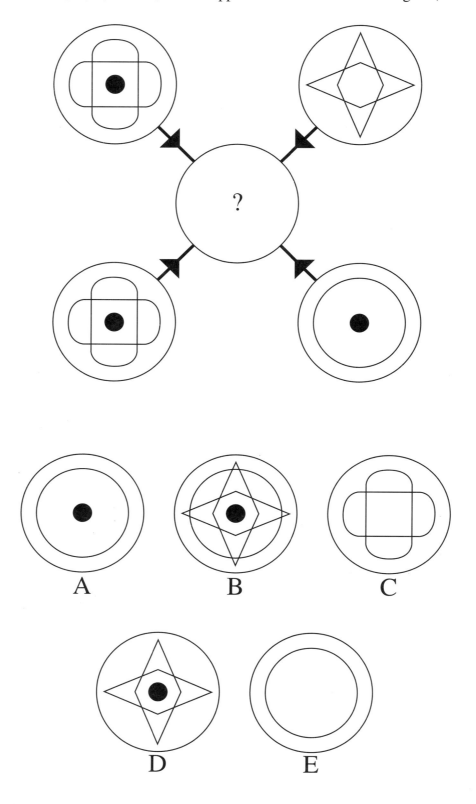

PUZZLE 20

What number should replace the ?

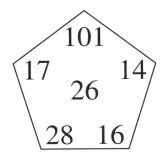

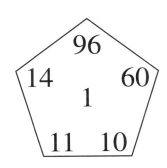

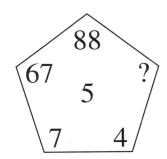

PUZZLE 21

Which number replaces the ?

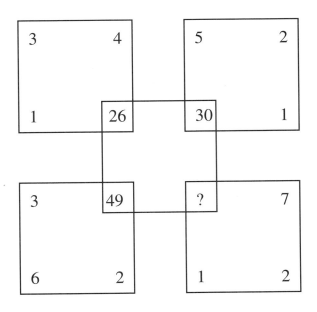

PUZZLE 22

Which letter is the odd one out in each shape?

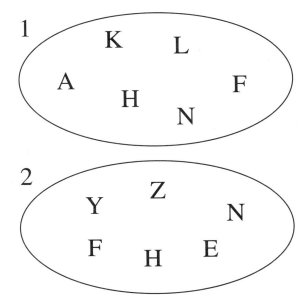

Which letter replaces the ?

B	D	G
D	O	K
T	A	P
K	C	?

Which number replaces the ?

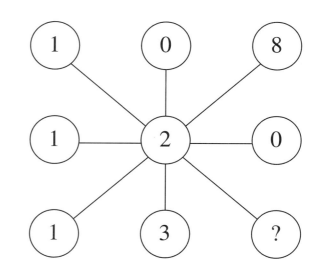

Which number replaces the ?

1

5   3

10

2   2

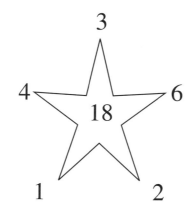

3

4   6

18

1   2

6

4   4

4

5   ?

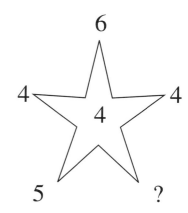

1. A

The figures at both ends move alternately, first the figure originally on the extreme left moves from left to right, then the figure originally on the extreme right moves from right to left.

2. 36 minutes

3. 3

So that all lines across and down total 10.

4.

Mary 44, Sally 66, Frank 99.

5. 913

The figures 3462891 are being repeated in the same order.

6. D

The figure on the left moves to the top of the pyramid and the other two figures remain at the bottom but change round.

7. A

So that in the large circle there are three mirror-image pairs of small circles.

8. Friday

9. 4

Looking across and down the middle number is the sum of the two other numbers above and below, divided by 2.

10. D

The two triangles without the dot remain in the same position. The triangle with the dot moves round clockwise, clamping itself to the nearest side of the remaining two triangles in turn.

11. 18

The two odd numbers are subtracted from the even number in each square.

12. 52

$6 \times 5 = 30 - 7 = 23$

$2 \times 8 = 16 - 9 = 7$

$14 \times 2 = 28 - 6 = 22$

$8 \times 7 = 56 - 4 = 52$

13. B

14. 0 2 1 8 7 9 6

15. A

1 is added to 2 to equal 3

4 is added to 5 to equal 6

like symbols disappear.

16. B

╱ stays same,

● moves 135° clockwise,

○ moves 135° clockwise,

✳ moves 180°.

17. (c) SLUGGISH

18. 156

$(12 \times 8) + (6 \times 14) - (2 + 8 + 10 + 4)$

19. E nearest to A contains • x •

20. 100

$$6 \times 7 = 42$$
$$12 \times 3 = 36$$
$$\frac{11}{89}$$

$$8 \times 2 = 16$$
$$5 \times 21 = 105$$
$$\frac{2}{123}$$

$$6 \times 7 = 42$$
$$14 \times 4 = 56$$
$$\frac{2}{100}$$

21. The other shapes are symetrical

22. - 48

23. (a)

24. 1A

25. (c) QUIBBLING

1. D

Looking round the octagon there are three pairs which have black/white reversal.

2.

A	B	C	D	E
C	D	E	A	B
E	A	B	C	D
B	C	D	E	A
D	E	A	B	C

3. 2.5 minutes

$$\frac{1}{5} + \frac{1}{4} - \frac{1}{20} = 0.2 + 0.25 - 0.05 = 0.4$$

$$\frac{1}{.4} = 2.5$$

4.
16

4. 16

5. L

There are two alternate sequences:

AbCdeFghiJklmnO

ZyXwvUtsrQponmL

6. 106

5 x 2, 1 x 6

7. 2573

In all the other numbers multiply the first and last digits to obtain the middle two.

8. B

The bottom figures fold up and across the top figure along the adjoining line.

9. 41

4 x 8 + 9

10. B, C, E

11. C

12. B

13. 14

14. 14

$(17 + 11 + 12) - (14 + 19) = 7$

$(18 + 16 + 15) - (6 + 5) = 38$

$(19 + 16 + 2) - (15 + 8) = 14$

15. (d) MEDLEY

16. FUTILE

17. E

1 is added to 2 to equal 3

4 is added to 5 to cancel 6 like symbols disappear.

18. 4 1/2 "

19. SCOFF

20.

The pentagon which has only 5 sides (odd number) The others have an even number of sides.

21. 1A

22. D = DIAMOND

H = 11

C = 8

D = 5

S = 1

23. 1 1/2

$$\frac{9}{72} \div \frac{36}{144} \div \frac{12}{36} =$$

$$\frac{1}{8} \div \frac{1}{4} \div \frac{1}{3} =$$

$$\frac{1}{8} \times \frac{4}{1} \times \frac{3}{1} = 1\ 1/2$$

24.

$$\frac{1}{13} \times \frac{1}{12} \times \frac{1}{11} \times \frac{1}{10} = \frac{1}{17160}$$

or

17159 to 1

25. 17 + 6 + 5 + 9 -

$(11 + 2 + 4 + 8) = 12$

1. C

2. G

Move five letters forward in the alphabet, then three back etc.

3. 3

4.

$3 \times 4 =$ 12 $6 \times 10 = 60$
$8 \times 6 =$ $\dfrac{48}{60}$

5. B

In all the others the top and third segments are the same.

6. 24 minutes

$40 \quad \times \quad \overline{6}$
$\qquad\qquad 10$

7. D

The dot moves to a different corner at each stage in a clockwise direction, and alternates in and out of the triangle, and also white/black.

8. 7

Start at 12 and move clockwise. Opposite segments as indicated in the diagram below are plus1, then plus 2 etc.

17	14	5	16
12			1
?			11
21	9	17	19

9. 99

Add the first digit of the previous number, then the second digit etc.

10. C

All segments are divided in half horizontally.

11. The pentagon has greatest number by 180°

Diamond 360°
Double triangle 360°
Pentagon 540°

12.

A   15
B   6
C   3
D   1

13. (d) CANTAR

14. 20 & 37 or 3

Opposite segments add to 27

Opposite segments are subtracted = 17

15. B

16. 6859

They are cube numbers

$16^3 \quad 17^3 \quad 18^3 \quad 19^3$

4096   4913   5832   6859

17. 32

$(9 + 8 + 13 + 6 + 10) - (6 + 7 + 1 + 8 + 4) = 20$

$(11 + 12 + 6 + 7 + 8) - (5 + 2 + 4 + 1 + 2) = 30$

$(17 + 14 + 12 + 9 + 7) - (11 + 7 + 3 + 2 + 4) = 32$

18. 156

$(12 \times 8) + (6 \times 14)$

$- (2 + 8 + 10 + 4)$

19. (b) 177

20. C

1 is added to 2 to equal 3.
4 is added to 5 to equal 6.
Like symbols disappear.

21. E = 36

add no. of side x 3

22. (e) OBVIOUS

23. 3C

24. 133

25.

Single 1 = 3.50
Pack 1 = 3.25
Saving = .25 $\dfrac{25}{3.50}$ = 7.1%

1. D

It has two small black circles, two small white circles, one larger black circle, two larger white circles (one with one of the small white circles inside it), and one large white circle (with one small white circle and one larger circle inside it).

2. Tuesday

3. 49.5

Add 3, then multiply by 3 etc

4. E

Carry forward only lines which appear in the same position in both previous circles, except that then, curved lines become straight and vice versa.

5.

A + E = B,

A + B = D,

D/E = C

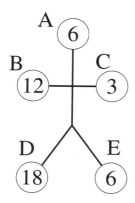

6. 1 hour

40 miles @ 40 mph = 1 hour;

60 miles @ 60 mph = 1 hour.

7. B

Only carry dots forward to the middle circle when they appear in the same position 3 times in the four surrounding circles.

8. 4

All lines across total 8.

9. All widgets have a hole in the middle.

10. B

In lines across multiply the number of circles to obtain the number in the third square. In lines down divide.

11. C

12. S

They are the 1st letters of the numbers 1-2-3-4-5-6.

13. (b) MARCASITE

14. MANACLE

15. D

A + C + E = SAME

B + F + G = SAME

16. 5.50

17. 5

(7 + 2 + 4) - (6 + 5) = 2

(9 + 1 + 7) - (2 + 2) = 13

(11 + 4 + 2) - (5 + 2) = 10

18. 152

19. 18 5/8

There are 2 series

16, 16 7/8, 17 3/4, 18 5/8

(+ 7/8 and - 3/4)

21, 20 1/4, 19 1/2

20. 3C

21. (c) A TURKISH TITLE

22. 4

The numbers are the number of letters in the question.

23. C

1 is added to 2 to equal 3

4 is added to 5 to equal 6

like symbols disappear.

24. B

25. 132

$$\frac{22}{\frac{2}{3}} = \frac{22}{\frac{1}{2}} = \frac{22}{\frac{4}{6}} \quad \frac{3}{6} \quad \frac{22}{\frac{1}{6}} = 22 \times 6 = 132$$

192

1. B

So that each horizontal and vertical line contains one each of the four different lines.

2. Q P H

The second set are the same distance from the end of the alphabet as the first set is from the beginning.

3. D

To complete every possible combination using three of the four different suits.

4. 630

Multiply by threequarters, one half, one quarter and repeat.

5. 2

Opposite numbers total 11.

6. L

Start at T and work down the left side adding 2 letters of the alphabet; move down the right side moving 2 letters back.

7. B

In all the others rounded figures are black and straight figures are white.

8. 4

A + D = B + E + C

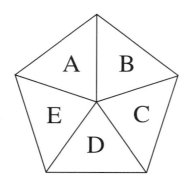

9. Jack

10. C

The dot moves from left to right alternating white/black; the triangle moves from right to left.

11. C

12. 15

26 - 10 = 16   14 - 7 = 7
31 - 9 = 22   12 - 5 = 7
$\overline{38}$ $\overline{14}$

21 - 9 = 12   17 - 10 = 7
11 - 2 = 9   9 - 1 = 8
$\overline{21}$ $\overline{15}$

13. 16

7 + 6 = 13   2 + 16 = 18   17 + 6 = 23
12 + 2 = 14   4 + 15 = 19   8 + 16 = 24
7 + 8 = 15   10 + 10 = 20   13 + 12 = 24
3 + 13 = 16   14 + 7 = 21   10 + 16 = 26
5 + 12 = 17   14 + 8 = 22   13 + 14 = 27

14. D

1 is added to 2 to equal 3

4 is added to 5 to cancel 6

like symbols disappear.

15. C

16. DEMODED

17. ELANCE

(The others are dances)

18. A

D is the same as G

B is the same as F

C is the same as E

19. 42

20. A

Where there is 1 line at a particular angle in (a), there are 2 at this angle in (b) and vice versa.

21. 29

Prime numbers 6th to 13th

22. 1000

The top circle contains the squares of 6-7-8-9-10

36-49-64-81-100

The bottom circle contains the cubes of 6-7-8-9

216-343-512-729-1000

23. (c)   A COAL MEASURE

24. (a)   PASTA

25. B

Each circle in the bottom large circle is a 90° rotation clockwise of a circle at the top.

1. C

The symbols move as in the first analogy, i.e. first to fourth, second to first, third to last, fourth to third, last to second.

2. 3

3. A

A new section appears at the beginning then the end alternately.

4. £48

5. 8

Add the numbers in the right and left squares to obtain the numbers in the middle square.

6. 10

There are 8 groups of three numbers round the diamond totalling 15;

$10 + 3 + 2 = 15$,

$8 + 2 + 5 = 15$ etc

7. P

Jump one letter then two letters etc : AbCdeFgHijKlMnoP

8. (d) BASKET

9. B

The circle goes to the top and the triangle flips in to the main figure.

10. 2

Each side of the triangle contains the numbers 1 - 9.

11. B

The outer segment moves 90° anti-clockwise at each stage, the middle segment moves 180° and the inner segment moves 90° clockwise.

12. F

The only one with a ball suspended from the shortest side.

13. F

14. 207

$72 + 3^2, + 4^2, + 5^2, + 6^2, + 7^2$

15. 20

$(7 + 26 + 17) -$
$(8 + 12 + 10) = 20$

16. D

1 is added to 2 to equal 3
4 is added to 5 to cancel 6
like symbols disappear.

17. (a) TIERCEL

The others are animals.

18. Answer B = 9

No. of angles =

    1 2 3 4 5

No. 1 3 5 7 9

19. E

A is the same as F

B is the same as G

C is the same as D

20. CHARNICO (drink)

The remainder are all

DANCES.

21. 90° F

22. (e) A WHIP

23. 48

Non-prime numbers between 38 and 48.

24. 8 KG

L	R
8 KG x 5 = 40	6 KG x 4 = 24
4 KG x 2 = 8	8 KG x 3 = 24
48	48

25. D

1. B

A is the same as E with black/white reversal, and C is the same as D.

2.

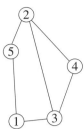

3. D

It goes anti-clockwise from outer to inner, the others going clockwise from outer to inner.

4. LMOP

All the others progress in the sequence, for example, K (+1)M(+1)OP.

5. 8

Numbers in the same shape of geometric figure all total 11.

6. 2415

7. 13 seats

37 people each paid £51.

8.

5

4

6

There are three sequences; 1,2,3,4,5 alternating top second; 0,1,2,3,4 alternating second third, and 2,3,4,5,6 alternating third first.

9. A

Every third figure is upturned and every fourth figure has a dot.

10. B

Every line has one upright diamond and one white star.

11. E

C is the same as A.

D is the same as G.

B is the same as F.

12. 89

Moving diagonally left to right each number decreases by the same amount as the number before.

13. A

14. 48

(6 + 7) x (5 - 2) = 39

(8 + 6) x (4 - 1) = 42

(10 + 2) x (6 - 2) = 48

15. A1

16. 7

Opposite numbers are multiplied and then the totals are added.

6	x	4	=	24
3	x	7	=	21
21	x	9	=	189
				234

11	x	9	=	99
2	x	7	=	14
8	x	8	=	64
				177

31	x	6	=	186
5	x	14	=	70
8	x	7	=	56
				312

17. B

2nd stack 3 drops out

3rd stack 3 drops out

4th stack 3 drops out

18. X

They are every 3rd letter in the alphabet with only straight lines.

A   miss E, F

H   miss I, K

L   miss M, N

T   miss V, W

X

19.

ALAN   16

BERTIE   27

CHARLIE   39

20. PONIARD, DAGGER

21.

46/27 ÷ 92/9

46/27 x 9/92 = 1/6

22.

VOWELS = 1

CONSONENTS = 3

ALSATION = 16

23. 7KG

LH	RH
6KG x 4 = 24	7KG x 4 = 28
8KG x 2 = 16	6KG x 2 = 12
40	40

24.

6/100 x 5/99 = 1/330

25. 8%

81 + 82 + 77 + 68 = 308

Amongst 100 pupils, this gives 3 losses each, and 4 losses to 8 pupils.

1. E

The figure moves through 180°, the black circle becomes a white star, the black diamond becomes a white circle and the white ellipse becomes a black square.

2. GC, 73

The numbers in the middle indicate the position of the numbers on the left from the beginning of the alphabet and the position of the numbers on the right from the end.

3. 35 (5 x 7)

4. J

All the others have one black dot in the vertical line and one white dot on the horizontal.

5. B

There is at least one black and white of each component in each horizontal and vertical line.

6. 23

Add 2 to the first 2 numbers, then 3 to the next 3 numbers etc.

7. 17

The number in each inner segment is the sum of the digits in the opposite outer segment, i.e. 9+8=17.

8. A

So that there is one dot in triangle/circle, and another dot in two triangles and a circle.

9.

4	6	8
7	T	2
1	3	5

10. 1.75

There are two alternate sequences, +1.25 and -2.75.

11. 14

12. B1

13. 6

$(5 \times 6 \times 7) \div (3 + 7) = 21$
$(4 \times 9 \times 2) \div (4 + 4) = 9$
$(6 \times 1 \times 9) \div (4 + 5) = 6$

14. 2

$(17+8+9)-(14+11+3)=6$
$(21+2+9)-(1+17+3)=11$
$(21+22+4) - (1+17+12)=2$

15. 44

$(9 \times 5) - (6 - 4)$
$(8 \times 7) - (9 - 3)$
$(7 \times 7) - (10 - 5)$

16. B

1 is added to 2 to equal 3.

4 is added to 5 to equal 6.

Similar symbols disappear.

17. 2KG

LH	RH
6KG x 4 = 24	12KG x 3 = 36
10KG x 2 = 20/44	2KG x 4 = 8/44

18. 88 years

19. B

20. E

A is the same as F

B is the same as G

C is the same as D

21.

$6^3 \div 36 = 6$

22. CORPULENT, LEAN

23. 28

24.

$3/10 \times 2/9 = 6/90 = 1/15$

25.

$52 \times 51 \times 50 \times 49 = 6,497,400$

1. D

So that each horizontal line contains the same line, with the dot in each of four positions.

2. 21   15

Each number is calculated using the two numbers below, In rows 2 and 4, take the difference of the two numbers below, in rows 3 and 5 add.

3. C

A dot in a circle and another dot in square/pentagon.

4. B

5. 24 minutes

6. 9

7. 4

$4 \times 19 = 76$

8. 13

9. 24

$6 \times 8 = 48/2$

10. 14

11. 28

12. E

13. A3

14. 2

$54+16=70÷(18+17)=2$

$90+9=99÷(19+14)=3$

$55+35=90÷(26+19)=2$

15. E

R is added to S to equal T

1 is added to 2 to equal 3

but similar symbols disappear.

16. 12

In 1st Hexagon opposite numbers add up to 36.

In 2nd Hexagon opposite numbers add up to 43.

In 3rd Hexagon opposite numbers add up to 32.

17. E

A is the same as G

B is the same as F

C is the same as D

18. 22

There are 2 series

(+6) 7-13-19-25

(+7) 8-15-22-29

19.

There are 2 series.

(+3) 17, 20, 23, 26,

(-6)   41, 35, 29, 23

20. $6 \times 5 = 30$

21. $180 = 6 \times 5 \times 4 \times 3 \times 2 \times 1/2 \times 2$

22. $(21 \times 14) - 3 - 3 = 288$

23. 1/36

24. 25

25. 9D

In each row, subtract the sum of the black cards from the sum of the red cards to give the value of the Heart on the right hand side.

1. 12

2. 1 minute

$(0.5 + 0.25) \times \frac{80}{60}$

3. 121

72-61 = 11; 11 x 11 = 121

4. E

Each horizontal and vertical line contains three different shaped stars, one of them is black, and one of them is without a moon.

5. Blue

The numbered coloured shirts coincide with the colours of the rainbow; blue is the fifth colour of the rainbow.

6. F

7. C

Looking across and down, the outer arc moves 90° clockwise at each stage, and the inner arc moves 90° anti-clockwise.

8. 2

Start at the top and then move right to left along the second row, then back left to right along the third row etc, repeating the numbers 36942.

9. 42867

Each number is the last three digits of the number above followed by the first two digits.

10. C

At each stage working from top to bottom two figures are inverted, and at each stage the dot moves from bottom to top and down again.

11.

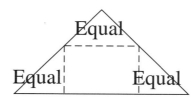

12. 18

8x8=64 Reversed = 46

5x5=25 Reversed = 52

4x4=16 Reversed = 61

7x7=49 Reversed = 94

6x6=36 Reversed = 63

9x9=81 Reversed = 18

13. A

14. B3

15. 8

(17 + 8 + 6) - (4 + 5 + 9) = 13

(16 + 1 + 5) - (8 + 7 + 2) = 5

(4 + 11 + 9) - (7 + 3 + 6) = 8

16. C

R is added to S to equal T

1 is added to 2 to equal 3

but similar symbols disappear.

17. 5

16 + 14 +10/4 = 10

37 + 15 + 8/10 = 6

29 + 18 + 3/10 = 5

18. £10

Ashtray £2

Chair £60

Table £240

19. 1018

Moving clockwise, double the previous number and add 6.

20. E

A is the same as C

B is the same as F

D is the same as G

21.

$8^2+7^2+6^2+5^2+4^2+3^2+2^2+1^2=204$

22. 168

$\frac{8 \times 7 \times 6 \times 5 \times 4 \times 3}{1 \times 2 \times 3 \times 4 \times 5 \times 6} \quad \times \quad \frac{6 \times 5 \times 4 \times 3 \times 2}{1 \times 2 \times 3 \times 4 \times 5}$

23. 72 @ £5.11 each = £

24. Black

25. QH

Numbering the cards Ace to King as 1-13, in each row, calculate the sum of the three left hand cards and the three right hand cards, and subtract the left hand total from the right hand total to give the value of the heart in the middle of the row.

1. B
The figure at the front goes to the back.

2. B   27
Starting top left, the letters progress through the alphabet, omitting 2 letters each time. The numbers represent the sum of the positions in the alphabet of the missing letters. When the end of the alphabet is reached return to A as if the letters were written in a circle.

3.
41
46
Start top left and move along the top row, then back along the second etc, in the sequence +2, -1, +3 etc.

4. B
In all the others left looking faces are frowning and right looking faces are smiling.

5. T
M   L
Start at the top and moving left-right then back right left, repeat the letters FJTLM.

6.   12684
Multiply each individual number by 2.

7. B
The large figure changes to white and rotates 90^{0} and goes inside one of the figures on the outside which increases in size and becomes black.

8.

15	6	10	14
11	4	8	2
13	1	T	12
3	9	5	7

9. B
There are two alternate sequences with a piece of each figure disappearing at each stage.

10.

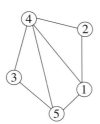

11. C

12. C2

13. 10

$$7 \times 6 = 42 \qquad 8 \times 6 = 48$$
$$- \; 6 \times 3 = \underline{18} \qquad - \; 4 \times 8 = \underline{32}$$
$$24 \qquad 16$$

14.   1 2/5
7/11÷14/22÷20/28=x
7/11 x 22/14 x 28/20 =
28/20 = 7/5
= 1 2/5

15.   19
Digits add up to 10
Others add up to 11

16.   70
+ 16 + jump 2 segments

17.   16
All the other numbers have the first digit larger than the second.

18.   29
Centre number is total of outside digits.

19.   F
A is the same as D
B is the same as E
C is the same as G

20.   260 m.p.h.

21.

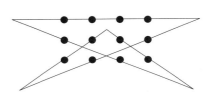

22.

$$\begin{array}{r} 4027 \\ \times 2 \\ \hline 8054 \end{array}$$

23.   593,775

24.   £315

25. D
1 is added to 2 to make 3
4 is added to 5 to make 6
but like symbols disappear.

1. D

The figure tumbles over onto a new side clockwise at each stage and also working clock-wise a different section is shaded at each stage.

2. 127

9 + 3 = 12, 7 x 1 = 7

3. C

4. T Q O

The first letters skip forward two places then one place from the front of the alphabet, and the second set skips two places then one place back from the end.

5. £495

6. A

7. 4

275986+342758=618744

8. MPR

Consecutive letters of the alphabet are placed in the same positions as in the two previous triangles.

9.

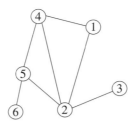

10. B

The little hand moves alternately two hours back then one hour forward and the big hand moves 10 minutes forward.

11. (d) GRENADA

12. 9

Two outside numbers added together make the opposite inside number.

13. C

14. 4

$$5x8=40$$
$$6x4=24$$
$$- \quad 16$$
$$8x6=48$$
$$9x4=36$$
$$- \quad 12$$
$$7x3=21$$
$$3x4=12$$
$$- \quad 9$$

15. A

It does not contain 37

16. B

17. CAPRICIOUS

FANCIFUL

18. 59 (prime number)

19. F

A is the same as E.

B is the same as D.

C is the same as G.

20. (c) MACAQUE (animal)

Rest are vegetables

21. (a) BARREN

22. 36 = 44 Modula 8

52 Mod 10 = 5 x 10, 2 x 1

52 Mod 8 = 6 x 8, 4 x 1

36 Mod 10 = 3 x 10, 6 x 1

36 Mod 8 = 4 x 8, 4 x 1

23. CARBON

They all contain birds

owl, roc, tit, emu

24. (c) FROZEN RAIN

25. D

1. D

When white dots appear in the same position twice in the first three pentagons they are transferred to the final pentagon. Black are transferred when they appear just once.

2. 8 people

Add $75 + 68 + 85 + 80 = 305$. This gives three items to all 100 people, and 4 items to five of them.

3. NXF

The other groups all have letters composed of the same number of lines. NXF has a mixture of 2 and 3.

4. C

Looking across and down, circles are only transferred to the final square when they appear in the same position in both previous squares, however, they then change from black to white and vice versa.

5. 14

The rest are all in a 1:3 ratio, 18/54, 24/72, 17/51, 12/36

6. C

The rectangle turns through $90°$, the diamond rotates through $180°$ and goes below the rectangle, and the ellipse rotates $90°$ and goes above the rectangle.

7. 50

$6 \times 15 = 90$

$7 \times 18 = 126$

$7 \times 20 = 140$

8. 413

Add the even numbers followed by the odd numbers.

9.

3	x	2	=	6
+		+		÷
5	-	3	=	2
=		=		=
8	-	5	=	3

10. 15

11. E

12. C

1 is added to 2 to equal 3

4 is added to 5 to equal 6

similar symbols disappear.

13. 9

Add digits to equal opposite corner $16 = 7$, $62 = 8$

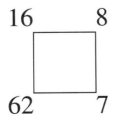

$$16 \qquad 8$$
$$62 \qquad 7$$

14. 156

$6 \times 17 = 102$	$8 \times 9 = 152$
$9 \times 18 = 162$	$21 \times 7 = 147$
$10 \times 21 = 210$	$12 \times 13 = 156$

15. $18 \div 6 \times 2$ ($\div$ or x) 1×10 $= 60$

16. (c) KNOB

17. PORTENT, INDICATION

18. R

The word spells camera. Each letter scores its position in the alphabet.

Ie. CAM $= 3+1+13=17$
     ERA $= 5+18+1=\overline{24}$
     -        Difference $\overline{7}$

19. (b) SQUALL

20. 1

6-4-7-2-1-1-2-7-4-6 repeats left to right

21. BREECHES

22.

131°

$$32°$$
$$99° \times 5 = 55°$$
$$9$$

23. B

The dot at the top alternates white black. The large circle at the bottom alternates white/striped/ black.The figure right in the centre alternates triangle/circle/square. The dot to the left of it alternates black/white. The dot to the right of it alternates striped/black/white.

24. (c) TIMID

25. C

1. B

A is the same as D with black/white reversal, as is C with E.

2. 18 1/4

There are 2 series

(+ 3 1/4) (-4 1/4)

18, 21 1/4, 24 1/2, 27 3/4

31, 26 3/4, 22 1/2, 18 1/4

3. C

The rest are all the same figure.

4. B

5. 12

The numbers in the bottom two circles are the sums of each pair of numbers in the top circles.

6. 14

All the rest have a mirror image pairing.

7. 2

$116 \times 3 = 348 \times 2 = 696$

8. 55

$2 + 3 = 5$ and $4 + 1 = 5$. Similarly $1 + 2 = 3$ and $5 + 3 = 8$.

9. 28

10. A

In all the others, one dot is in one circle and the other dot is in two circles. In A both dots are in two circles.

11. B

12. E,G

A is the same as H

B is the same as F

C is the same as D

13. 44

$(8 \times 5) - (6 + 6) = 28$

$(9 \times 8) - (7 + 7) = 58$

$(8 \times 7) - (9 + 3) = 44$

14. D

1 is added to 2 to equal 3

4 is added to 5 to equal 6

But similar symbols disappear.

15. 2917 (B)

7x4=28	5x4=20
3x7=21	4x6=24
2x9=18 (17)	7x2=14
8x7=56	6x9=54
6x3=18	2x9=18
1x9=09	8x8=64

16. 41

$6 + 10 = 16$, $16 + 8 = 24$,

$24 + 8 = 32$, $32 + 9 = 41$,

$41 + 7 = 48$, $48 + 6 = 54$,

$54 + 2 = 56$, $56 - 50 = 6$

17. 22

$(7 + 9) \times 4$	$= 64$
$(8 + 5) \times 5$	$= 65$
$(2 + 4) \times 11$	$= 66$
$(5 + 6) \times 2$	$= 22$

18. 6

$7-1=6$

$6 \times 7=42$

19. (e) COWBOY

20. DISSIPATE, SAVE

21. 107

Add digits i.e.

$44+8=52$,

$52+7=59$ etc.

22. .1666

23. (e) WHEELS

24. (a) GOLD COIN

25. (d) DIRIIUM

(Iridium, Mineral)

The others are colours

Maroon, Pinkish, Russet, Bluish.

1. B

Alternating boxes on horizontal and vertical lines rotate by 90°.

2.
Add 96347, 10496, 21221 and 34628 = 162692.
Divide by 4 = 40673
40673 is the number of votes received by the successful candidate.
Therefore, the second received 30177 (40673-10496).
The third received 19452 (40673-21221)
and the fourth received 6045 (40673-34628).

3. G

4.

A B C D E F E C A F B D
7 4 2 1 6 3 6 2 7 3 4 1

5. D

A new parallelogram is added at each stage, the previous parallelograms flipping outside then inside the hexagon.

6. ETFNJDOK

The letters in the previous rectangle are reversed, and the letter third from last is discarded.

7. 119.30

Add the last two digits only each time i.e. 109.6 + 9.6 = 119.2

8. D

The previous figures move down at each stage and a new symbol is added at the top.

9.

33   34   34   35

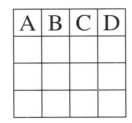

A + C = A
B + C = B
A + D = C
B + D = D

10. F

Only symbols which are common to the first two squares in each horizontal and vertical line are carried forward to the final square.

11. D

12. B+F
A same as E.
G same as D.
C same as H.

13. 110
(17 x 8) - 6 = 130
(11 x 7) - 4 = 73
(13 x 9) - 7 = 110

14. D
1 is added to 2 to equal 3
4 is added to 5 to cancel 6
like symbols disappear.

15. 7
Opposite numbers = total digits
93=12   29=11   71=8
37=10   36=9   55=10
67=13   37=10   43=7
A   B   C

16. 108

17.

18.
They all carry coins within the words
DIME, RAND, MARK, CENT, RIAL, SOU

19.

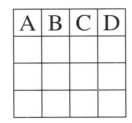

20. 10H
In each column of the diagram, the sum of the three cards is always 20, and one of each suit is used in each row.

21. C
Adding up the digits on each watch face, from left to right, thetotal increases by 5 each time.

22. 49
(7 x 9) - 6   = 57
(8 x 6) - 7   = 41
(9 x 3) - 4   = 23
(10 x 6) - 11   = 49

23. (c) A FISH

24. Square of 19

19   7
19   7
171   49
190   7
361   343

25.
99/16 ÷ 11/4 = 99/16 x 4/11
= 2 1/4

1. D

It is a curved figure in a straight figure. All the others are straight figures inside curved figures.

2. 2548

The rest have their digits in ascending order.

3. E

4.

623 - 36 - 18

847 - 224 - 16

726 - 84 - 32

i.e. 6 x 2 x 3 = 36, 3 x 6 = 18

5. K

There are three sequences.

ABC (top/second/top lines)

BEH (second/last/second lines)

CGK (bottom/top/bottom lines)

6. 114213

Each line describes the numbers in the line above, starting with the lowest numbers first i.e. 212223 has 1 x 1, 4 x 2, 1 x 3.

7. C

Arcs increase by quarter circles and a new quarter circle starts where the previous arc ends.

8.

25, 28, 27, 24, 26

9. 11

Add all the numbers above and divide by 2.

10. B

So that each line and column contains 10 dots.

11. D

12. AC

Start in the top left corner, and move in a clockwise spiral around the diagram, towards the centre. The value of each card increases by 4 each time. To calculate the suits of each card, start at the top left and move in an anti-clockwise spiral towards the centre, following the sequence Hearts, Clubs, Diamonds, Spades.

13.

$$\frac{5}{32} \quad \frac{1}{2} + \frac{1}{4} \times \frac{3}{8} - \frac{7}{16} = \frac{1}{2} + \frac{3}{32} - \frac{7}{16} = \frac{16+3}{32} - \frac{14}{32}$$

14. B G

A is the same as H

C is the same as F

D is the same as E

15.

(9+8)x3 = 51

(6+5)x8 = 88

(7+1)x6 = 48

(5+2)x9 = 63

16. E

1 is added to 2 to equal 3

4 is added to 5 to equal 6

Like symbols disappear.

17. C

All odd numbers except for C = 54.

18. R

sequence is

D E̸ F G̸ H̸ I J̸ K

L̸ M N̸ Ø P̸ Q̸ R

19. (e) ENVIRONMENT

20. (a) UGLINESS

21. 11

$9^2 - 1^2 = 80$

$7^2 - 3^2 = 40$

$6^2 - 5^2 = 11$

22. 41

Column A	Odd numbers
Column B	Even numbers
Column C	Square numbers in sequence
Column D	Prime numbers in sequence

23. (a) TOBACCO

24. (a) OATMEAL

25. 470, 10

(7+8=15) 78+15 x10 = 930

(2+9=11) 29+11x10 = 400

(3+7=10) 37+10x10 = 470

1. D

2.
196 - 114 - 44
376 - 222- 44
487 - 336 - 198
19 x 6 = 114; 11 x 4 = 44

3.
15   5
61-56 = 5
15/3 = 5

4. D
The large circle moves two clockwise, the small white circle moves two anti-clockwise, the triangle moves one anti-clockwise and the black circle moves one anti-clockwise.

5. 3
5 + 11 =16; square root of 16 = 4, so 2 + 7 = 9 and square root of 9 = 3.

6. O
The sequences occur looking across letters in the same position in each pentagon. Two move forward by missing 2 letters in the alphabet and three move by missing 2 back.

7. B
The others are made up of three identical figures.

8. 13654:
ABCDE - CDEBA

9. 6
The number in the middle is the average of the numbers surrounding it.

10. D
Horizontally and vertically the sequence runs - add one line, keep same number of lines, add one line etc.

11. A

12. 18
The inner numbers are 3 times the difference between the outer numbers.

13. (e) COAX

14. (b)   30

$$(15) \ (4^2) \quad = x \ (2^3)$$
$$15 \ x \ \ 16 \quad = x \ (8)$$
$$240 \quad = 8x$$
$$30 \quad = x$$

15.

6		
1	2	3
4	5	6
7	8	9

16. D
1 is added to 2 to equal 3
4 is added to 5 to cancel 6
like symbols disappear.

17. 28
(9 + 8) x 1 = 17
(5 + 6) x 3 = 33
(6 + 7) x 4 = 52
(3 + 11) x 2 = 28

18. A
Each circle is made up by adding together the two circles below but like symbols disappear.

19. 0
Each circle adds to 89.

20. 69p
Each letter represents the number of the letter counting from z = 1, y = 2, x = 3, etc.

21. 15507
Each number x3

22. 9

546	664	527
+241	+227	+127
787	891	654

23. 57

24. (c) ANAPURNA

25. 7
98 ÷ 7 = 14 reverse 41

1. D

The rest are the same figure.

2. 9

Each diagonal line increases by 2 as shown below.

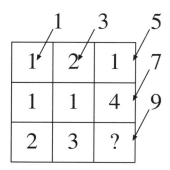

3. WTUV

The rest are consecutive letters of the alphabet in the sequence

LMNO   OMLN
1 2 3 4   4 2 1 3

4. 5 revolutions

Take the lowest number (lowest common multiple) that all three cogs will divide into, in this case 60.

Then divide by the largest wheel i.e. 60/12 = 5 revolutions.

5. E

6. 89

48/3 = 16, 72/9 = 8, so 24/3=8 and 45/5=9

7. 8.6

There are two alternate sequences, +1.65 and +1.92.

8. D

Looking across each line and down each column, any lines which are common to the first two squares are not carried forward to the final square.

9. B

So that one square in each horizontal line contains all the lines in the other three squares.

10. 132.375

Add, multiply by and subtract 1.5 in turn.

11. L

Representing each letter by its position in the alphabet, and multiplying the outside number you obtain the inside numbers.

C L D   3   12   4
F L B   6   12   2
E Y E   5   25   5

12. B1

13. A

14. A

1 is added to 2 to equal 3
4 is added to 5 to equal 6
but similar symbols disappear.

15. 28

$(7 \times 4) + 6 = 34$
$(9 \times 1) + 7 = 16$
$(8 \times 3) + 9 = 33$
$(6 \times 4) + 4 = 28$

16. 0

$(6 + 11 + 2) - (5 + 4) = 10$
$(9 + 3 + 6) - (5 + 4) = 9$
$(11 + 3 + 14) - (10 + 0) = 18$

17. ERUDITION,
    ILLITERACY

18. 8C

Starting on the left and moving right, the value of each cards increases by 6, 7, 8, 9 and 10, with odd numbered cards as Hearts, and even cards as Clubs.

19. 468

$3^3 + 2^3 = 35$
$4^3 + 5^3 = 189$
$5^3 + 7^3 =$

20. PARADISE
(pair of dice)

21. 69

$8 \times 12 = 96$ reverse 69
$3 \times 32 = 96$ reverse 69

22. 760

In all the other numbers, the sum of the first two digits equals the third.

23. 30

As you move down, numbers increase by 7, 6, 5, 4 and 3.

24. K

In each row the central figure equals the sum of the alphabetical value of the left hand letter and the reverse alphabetical value of the right hand letter.

25. R

Starting in the top left segment of each circle, and moving clockwise, double the value of each letter and subtract 2 to give the value of the next letter around.

1. 1 chance in

1105 or $\dfrac{6 \times 5 \times 4}{152 \ 51 \ 50} = \dfrac{1}{1105}$

1104 to

2. 13 cats killed 23 rats (both these factors are prime numbers).

3. 94.75

There are two alternate sequences, -1.75 and -2.25.

4. D

The main figure faces the other way at each stage and the line moves down a quarter then back to the top again at each stage.

5. 77

Add the sum of the digits of the previous number each time.

6. 35

16 + 22 + 24 = 62; 3 x 9 = 27;

62 - 27 = 35

7. C

The figures are in the same order but go in the opposite direction as the other options.

8. J

From the middle letter start at N and work clockwise. The letters skip +1, -1, +2, -2, +3, -3, +4, -4.

9.

Frasier 46,

Niles 42,

Daphne 34

10. B

Horizontally and vertically, add one dot outside and inside the diamond until there are four and then remove on dot.

11. A

12. 46

Starting at 21   1-4-3-2 are added in succession.

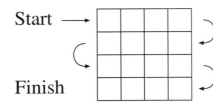

13.

6x3 (to the power of 9) =

6x19683 = 118098

14.

60 (MOD 8) = 48 (MOD 10)

33 (MOD 8) = 27 (MOD 10)

15. 476

$6^3 - 4^2 = 200$

$7^3 - 5^2 = 318$

$8^3 - 6^2 = 476$

16. C2

17. 24

(6 x 7) - 8 = 34,

(9 x 5) - 11 = 34,

(12 x 6) - 26 = 46,

(8 x 4) - 12 = 20,

(6 x 6) - 12 = 24

18. 40

16+11+29=29+27

4x18+51=6+67

18+19+5=40+2

19. B

1 is added to 2 to equal 3

4 is added to 5 to cancel 6

like symbols disappear.

20. (D)

⊙ remains,

◯ moves opposite,

● moves opposite,

⬤ moves to centre and returns.

21. L

T has 8 right angles

L has 6 right angles

O has 8 right angles

C has 8 right angles

U has 8 right angles

J has 8 right angles

22. 14

In each row, subtract 1 from the left and central numbers, and multiply together to give the right hand number.

23. Z

Moving in diagonal lines, from top left to bottom right, letters increase in value by 4 each time.

24. Z

Starting at C and moving clockwise, letters increase in value by 5, then 4 alternately.

25. 132

All other numbers contain the digit 4.

1. F
Looking across and down the number of sides in the figures increases by 1 in each square.

2. H
Start at the top left corner and spiral round the perimeter skipping 2 letters in the alphabet, then going back one letter alternately. Finish in the centre square.

3. D
The only one with two successive stars.

4. MNOP
Start at A and miss one letter before the next line, then miss two letters then finally three letters i.e.
AbCDefGHIjklMNOP

5. P
Looking across and down omit 1 letter then 2 letters then 3 letters in successive rows and columns.

6. C
Start at the top left-hand square and work along the top and then back along the second row etc., in the sequence white circle, black circle, triangle.

7. 24
27 + 21 = 48; 4 x 6 = 24; 48 - 24 = 24

8. 13.25
There are two sequences, +3.75 and +2.75.

9. B
All figures move one side clockwise. Then figures outside go inside and black figures become white and vice versa.

10. JLO
So that all connected lines contain the same letters.
JKLMNOP

11. 7
2nd line is subtracted from the 1st line to obtain the 3rd line.

12. A

● moves 1 corner clockwise
• moves 1 corner clockwise
○ moves 1 corner anti-clockwise
╱ moves 1 line clockwise
╲ moves 1 corner anti-clockwise

13. 97
$\quad 8 \times 9 = 72$
$- \quad 4 + 8 = 12$
$\overline{\qquad 60}$
$\quad 11 \times 7 = 77$
$- \quad 6 + 5 = 11$
$\overline{\qquad 66}$
$\quad 13 \times 9 = 117$
$- \quad 5 + 4 = 9$
$\overline{\qquad 108}$

14. A1

15. D
No. of lines
A 6
B 8
C 5
D 6
E 7

16. (b) RUBBER

17.
They all carry a boy's name
ALF, ELI, HAL, LEN, NED, PAT

18. 32
Add reversed numbers.

61	76	11	16
41	5	14	12
7	12	7	4
109	93	32	32

19. B

20. 5
101-26=17+14+28+16
96-1=14+11+10+60
88-5=67+7+4+5

21. 54
In each square, the sum of the squares of the three outer numbers equal the number bounded by the central square.

22. 1=L, 2=E
All other letters in each oval are written with 3 strokes of the pen.

23. V
Starting in the top left, and moving in a clockwise spiral towards the centre, letters increase in value by 2, 3, 4, 5...etc.

24. 2
Reading each row as a 3 digit number, rows follow multiples of 123 (108, 120, 132).

25. 1
In each star, multiply the left and right hand numbers together, then subtract the upper and two lower numbers to give the value in the centre of the star.